Here
I Stand

Here I Stand
One City's Musical History

By Sonya Bernard-Hollins
Graphic Design by Sean Hollins

Fortitude Graphic Design & Printing
Kalamazoo, Michigan

Published & Designed by Fortitude Graphic Design and Printing
in collaboration with Season Press LLC

Library of Congress Control Number
2016915091

Library of Congress Cataloging-in-Publication
Data:
Hollins, Sonya.
Here I Stand: One City's Musical History/ Sonya Hollins and
Sean Hollins
1. History-African American 2. Music Industry
3. Battle Creek, Michigan.

Includes Index.
ISBN Paperback: 978-0-9741611-0-5
ISBN Hardcover: 978-0-9977136-6-4

FOURTH EDITION
10 9 8 7 6 5 4
Season Press LLC
PRINTED IN THE UNITED STATES OF AMERICA

To
God, who has blessed me with the gifts, which have made it possible for me to share the stories of the musicians of Battle Creek with the world.

My husband Sean, who has motivated me from the beginning of this project with his love and awesome talent as a graphic designer.

Our sons Edward and Shamiel, who have been on this musical journey since the beginning. And to our daughters Syann and Sasha, who have come into the world after the first edition of this book was published in 2003.

S.H.

CONTENTS

INTRODUCTION

Some days you make plans in the hope that things will go exactly as you envision. But when things take a turn in an unexpected direction, what do you do? Do you panic, or sit back and let nature take its course?

I chose to let nature sing its predestined song on an exceptionally warm and breezy Saturday afternoon on April 7, 2001. In the small farm community of Climax, Michigan, Jim Cummings, musician, and owner of Soundstage I Productions, opened his beautiful home as a backdrop for an interview session. Musicians he had admired, worked with, or would (like my husband Sean and I) meet for the first time, were invited to participate.

The musicians all had a connection. They had at one time or another performed in Battle Creek at the once popular club call The El Grotto Lounge. We intended to meet men who would introduce me to the world I could only live vicariously through their stories of stage, stardom.

A few weeks earlier, I had sent letters to nearly a dozen musical artists to invite them to an interview where they could be recorded and interviewed for an upcoming book. As a reporter at the *Battle Creek Enquirer,* I had heard that some of the musicians who first appeared on the stage of the tiny club went on to achieve national–and for some worldwide success.

Several articles had been written throughout the years on the triumphs of a few of them. Others, however, had never been interviewed and had passed into obscurity. They would now have a chance to share their story.

We came equipped with sub sandwiches, Sean's famous cavity-inducing Kool-Aid, two video cameras, and four rolls of 35-mm film. I planned to introduce myself to those in the group whom I'd never met, and then distribute forms for them to fill out of the vital information of their career. I would interview each guest, thank them for coming, and use what I gathered to compile a book for some time in the future.

But, as the time approached for the interviews to begin, only two musicians had shown up. What happened? Did the others feel the interviews weren't worth their time? Did they forget? Did they get lost?

As we waited, Cummings gave us a tour of his beautiful home, which also contained state-of-the art recording studios. The hardwood floors and antique store counter in the sitting room were beautifully restored to resemble its original interior when it served as the town's general store and bank.

Then, it started to happen. Men began to float in one by one. They were armed with treasures in brown paper bags, neatly cradled folders, and photo albums of priceless pictures snug behind plastic covered pages.

"Man, I didn't know you were coming! I haven't seen you since, when, 1970?" one said to another. Soon they were telling stories of a once explosive culture of live music in Battle Creek. These guys remembered possessing the magic to captivate an enthusiastic audience and hold them in the palms of their hands. Before sports became a means of success for

African Americans, music was one of the most glamorous ways to escape poverty or menial jobs. These men took hold of the dream to see their name gleam in lights on a marquee and hit the perfect pitch to make sold-out crowds scream for more.

As we sat in Jim's home on that spring day in 2001, that magic was rekindled in the stories that took them back more than forty years. They shared their stories as time stood still. Mental flashbacks were like reels of a movie where the finger-poppin', leg shakin', head bobbin' music these men performed came to life.

During a four-hour ride down memory lane, they glowed over their scrapbooks, laughed at the fashions and hair styles once proudly sported, and reminisced about those who had passed on, but were immortalized in the photos. Not much had gone according to my detailed plan for one-on-one private interviews. Chairs had been rearranged into a semicircle, and everyone took turns as they shared memories. Each respected the others' time, but took the liberty to jump in to bring up a funny memory or share a sad story that related to the tale of the moment.

The men who gathered here were graced with a bit more time on earth, and one even said he felt there was still something missing in his life; something he had yet to finish. After the interviews, I couldn't let them leave without giving me a sample of what they bragged about–their music. I was born as the Do Wop era came to a close. By the time I was born, many of these men had left the stage and had settled down to marry, get a well-paying job, and raise a family.

I wanted them to go back, to the days before they had to punch a clock. I wanted them to take me back to the years when their hearts, and a drummers rat-a-tat-tat beat as the sun set and the crowd came to party.

Jim took the hint and led us all downstairs to his recording studio. We didn't have to twist any arms. Before we knew it, Sonny Holley warmed up the Hammond organ. Bill "Sticks" Nicks adjusted was the drum set in the corner, and Bobby Holley grabbed the microphones and tested—one, two, three. What we experienced was a raw talent, unleashed after years of being sequestered by life. It was a moment I will never forget.

After sweating to the oldies for more than an hour, they proved to me–and themselves that they still had "it." When the session ended they exchanged phone numbers and promised to keep in touch. They carefully repacked their memories into brown shopping bags with the gentleness of a mother swaddling a newborn baby. Those memories would go back in there for now, along with the 45 rpm records, complete with that yellow thing in the middle that kept the record steady on the turntable.

No one remembers when they last played the records or the last time they even had a working record player. But that didn't matter. These were priceless jewels to them, never to be parted with in their lifetime. One man said of his many treasured photographs, "I keep these things to remind me of how things use to be, not how they are."

But what they used made them who they are today. To deny that would be to deny themselves and the influence they had on music in their hometown, and the world. People rarely realize what a person has contributed to the world until after they are gone. Then, it's too late to give them him a pat on the back or acknowledge that he made a difference. We then often attempt to recreate him and his experiences for the history books.

As the men go back to work for the government, operate their own businesses, or work in various fields, they will never forget those days on stage. A younger generation, however, has no idea what these men have contributed to the world of music. As they board a bus and clink their coins into the bus changer, they don't know that the man driving the bus traveled the world, making crowds roar.

Unfortunately, many of the key artists we discussed during the meeting are gone and couldn't share their own story. Fortunately, many others were still around. Here are their stories as they remember them, along with the history of the city that served as the stage of their lives.

A Melody

By Jayda Craig

There's a song in my heart that I wish to sing to the world,
so I write it.

As the words are written, a spirit of inspiration intervenes,
transpiring into a chorus,
so I write it.

Experiences of joy, experiences of sorrow,
things of the past and hope for tomorrow
complete the lyrics and unifies the versus,
so I write it.

And I write it with Love,
I write it with Truth,
I write it with Wisdom...

and soon it becomes a song
in someone else's heart,
and that's when it becomes
A Melody.

Part 1
Battle Creek's Early Years

Washington Heights - 1915
New homes on Greenwood Avenue.
~Sonya Hollins Collection~

It had already become famous as a place where hidden fortunes lay dormant, ready to spring into existence. I little thought then it would be my future home, but I was much pleased with it and its prospective advantages.

These are the words of abolitionist Erastus Hussey as written in a letter to his friend, Anson D.P. VanBuren about Battle Creek (1875). - *Martich Collection-Willard Library*

A Place of Promise

Melvin Evans' eyes sparkle and his posture straighten as he goes into storyteller mode. He, more than anyone, knows about the American Dream. He saw it in action as his sister Helen, and her husband Robert "Snap" Montgomery, took a hurtful episode of racism and turned it into a story of success.

Snap moved from Culp, Illinois to Battle Creek in 1926 during the Depression Era, for a better way of life. He served in the U.S. Navy during World War II and eventually secured a job at Kellogg's cereal factory. He worked hard, each day, and like some men, left work to unwind with a drink at a local tavern.

After Snap finished his drink at the white-owned establishment, he paid his tab and prepared to leave. He heard a glass explode into pieces. The bartender had taken Snap's empty glass from the bar and broke it. He would not chance any of his white customers drinking from the same glass as a Negro.

Snap was hurt, embarrassed, infuriated. He stormed home and told his wife. After a long night of discussion, they had a plan. It was a plan that would forever change their lives and set them up to change the lives of others for decades to come.

The historical archives of any city, large or small, contains documents and photographs, all of which are pieces to a puzzle. One piece could be the town's first survey plans. Another piece may tell of an event that helped bring the town notoriety or shame. The most important piece of any town's history, however, is its people; the natives, the pioneers, and those who would contribute to what the future would become.

Battle Creek, like most areas in the United States, existed before the pioneers staked their claims to the land. The area was home to Native Americans who resided there long before Columbus "discovered" America in 1492. Battle Creek, like the places many pioneers ventured toward, was a place of new hope, new dreams, and new opportunities.

For the Michigan natives, the building of the Erie Canal changed life as they had known it. In 1825, after eighteen years of construction, the canal stretched 363 miles across New York from Albany to Buffalo. The link facilitated the transportation of passengers and freight between the eastern seaboard and Michigan ports.

It was built at a time when the country was in turmoil over the position of slavery. The business of trading slaves across the world for other products and services began with the Portuguese and Spanish in the 1400s. Dutch, English, and French later joined in the business, to be followed by the American colonies. Traders used the Transatlantic Trading System to ship African slaves to the Caribbean in return for native goods such as molasses. Molasses was turned into rum, which was traded in Africa for more slaves. This was one of many trading routes which shipped more than ten million slaves across the Atlantic Ocean from the 15th well into the 19th century.

In 1833, the British Empire outlawed slavery and the trade circle tightened. In America, some slaves risked death to escape slavery. Evangelical Christians in the North believed slavery was a sin, and that slaveholders were contravening God's will by keeping slaves in bondage. Soon abolitionists began to take action.

Two years later, former slave Nat Turner gathered an army of more than sixty slaves to revolt against slavery. They killed fifty-seven whites on plantations around his birthplace of Southampton County, Virginia before he was caught and executed. His uprising was not the first initiated by slaves but energized the anti-slavery movement.

The opening of the Erie Canal allowed those opposed to slavery to move deeper into the Midwest and farther away from the southern states. The abolitionists, including many Quakers, settled in Michigan and became instrumental in creating safe grounds for those who sought to escape the bondage of slavery in the south.

Erastus Hussey left Cayuga County, New York in 1836 to establish himself and his family in a small town in Michigan. During the same time, brothers Abraham, Joseph, and Issac Merritt also left Syracuse, New York for a new life in Michigan along with thousands of others to embark on the newly found state.

The Merritt brothers fought through the thick unsettled forests of Michigan toward the settlement where they made a claim on six hundred acres at $1.25 an acre. They then returned to New York to bring their families to their new home.

In addition to his family, Issac Merritt brought along his coachman, Lewis Jackson, a free black man. Stephen Valentine arrived in the settlement around the same time and brought his maid, a black woman named Louisa Heart. Jackson and Heart were the first of African descent to live in the new settlement.

Hundreds of new landowners soon convened to create an official name for their thriving town, which contained a general store, a blacksmith, a foundry, and many log homes. A total of sixty people voted for the name, Waupakisco, a native (Indian) name for river, water, or battle. Legend had it that earlier settlers fought a bloody battle with the native tribe at the location of the town's river. Knowing that history, 315 of the town's people voted for the name, Battle Creek, the English translation of Waupakisco.

With a new name, thriving businesses and settled land, the settlers began to marry and start families. Jackson and Heart married in 1840, and in 1842 had the first black child born in the town, John Henry Jackson. The couple, although free in New York, was more secure in Michigan as racial tensions began to brew in New York. The safety of Michigan, where slavery was not enforced, was something others of African descent–freed or enslaved–would soon seek.

The Underground Railroad

Soon the escape route from slave states to free states become known as the Underground Railroad. Although not actually part of a train rail system, the Underground Railroad was a group of abolitionists who worked together in secret to move "passengers" long distances toward freedom.

In Battle Creek, Hussey and many others in the city shared anti-slavery views. It was his reputation as a leader and successful store owner that led John Cross of Indiana to suggest that Hussey take charge of the Underground Railroad in Battle Creek.

Five other men in the town, including a black man, Samuel Strothers, also were a part of this effort. Strothers was a charter member of Battle Creek's Second Baptist Church, which was established in 1849. (He later founded Strothers Lodge #3 Free and Accepted Masons of Michigan in 1864.) They learned that the estimated 1,000 slaves who escaped from Kentucky each year, had the most success toward freedom. Those in states farther south had a more challenging feat in attempts to reach freedom because of borders that were heavily monitored by bounty hunters.

Slave owners began to hear of more successful escapes. In fear of losing their "property," they sold their slaves farther south where the chance of escape north was remote. Those in the deep south sometimes ran into the swamps of Florida to join the Seminole Indians, or attempted to stow away on boats bound for the Caribbean where slavery was outlawed in 1831. Those in Texas sought freedom by heading into Mexico, which had banned slavery in 1821.

The international slave trade was abolished in 1807 and had reduced the number of imported slaves. This lead to more slave trading within the United States. Traders sold slaves as a financial investment with little regard to their marital or family status. The marriage of slaves to one another was binding and existed only at the whim of slave owners. With that, the fear of separation led many slaves to do everything in their power to flee with their entire family to free states.

One man took that risk. Adam Crosswhite was born in 1799 to a slave mother and her white slave owner. He had already been separated from his own mother and sold to another plantation. Now, with a wife and four children, he felt escape was his only hope for them to remain together.

In 1847 they escaped, and in Michigan, helped by Quakers of Cass County. They left the area just months before the historic Kentucky Raid on the town for fugitive slaves. By this time Crosswhite and his family moved through the Battle Creek Underground Railroad to settled in Marshall, the county seat known for its elegant homes and hotels. After years away from the plantation, bounty hunter Francis Troutman discovered the Crosswhites' location. The town members united to help the family escape to nearby Jackson to smuggle them to Canada for safety.

Although the family was never captured, Troutman returned to sue the townspeople who aided in the planned escape. The case was tried in Detroit in 1848 and resulted in a hung jury. A second trial awarded Troutman $1,926. This incident, known as the Crosswhite Affair, and the Cass County Incident (Kentucky Raid) are believed to be instrumental in the passage of the Fugitive Slave Law of 1850, which made it illegal to aid slaves to freedom.

Freedom for All

By 1850, thirty-four of the town's 1,064 residents were black. Slavery was still in effect in the country, but there was a glimmer of hope that one day, the ills of slavery would come to an end. That hope encouraged with the granting of freedom to slaves in West India. On August 1, 1853, the black community in Battle Creek celebrated that milestone with the city's first Emancipation Day.

"Every colored person in Battle Creek was out for a good time," according to an article in the city's *Weekly Journal*. Leaders in the community such as William Casey, John Gaines, S. Johnson, J. Weaver, B. Allen, and Thomas Henderson, organized the event. A processional began at the School House (African Methodist Episcopal church) at 9 a.m. They marched down to the village and then returned for picnic and fellowship.

The celebration became an annual event. Black citizens celebrated the Emancipation of those in the West Indies, which was an inspiration that slaving would end, one day, in their own country. That hope was not be longed lived. During the 1860 national convention, Democrats (mainly of the south) and Republicans debated the expansion of slavery in the western territories. The northerners won. Southerners walked out of convention. Abraham Lincoln won the presidency despite the fact that he received very few votes south of the Mason-Dixon Line. The threat of war began to brew.

Most slave states soon seceded from the Union. Missouri, Kentucky, and part of Virginia (later to become West Virginia in 1863) were slave states but did not join with the other Confederate States. In 1861 the Civil War had began with the attack on Fort Sumter, South Carolina by Confederate soldiers.

Lincoln believed that the war was to preserve the Union. However, radical Republicans wanted to save the Union and destroy slavery. Once the war began slaves from Virginia escaped by the thousands to Union army encampments. The encampments were safe havens where Union soldiers did not condone slavery. Union soldiers considered these slaves property of the Union and did not return them to their slaveholders.

In 1862 Lincoln outlawed slavery in the District of Columbia, and that summer the Second Confiscation Act passed, declaring all slaves considered contraband to be forever free. On September 22, 1862, Lincoln signed the Emancipation Proclamation to free all slaves in the areas that were in active rebellion effective January 1, 1863. The 13th Amendment would later free all slaves.

The 895 men of the First Michigan Colored Infantry Regiment (later called the 102nd Regiment United States Colored Troop) were mustered into service on February 14, 1864. By the end of the war in 1865, 1,673 blacks were enlisted. While the black soldiers at first received low or no wages, some eventually received $10 a month (compared to $13 a month for white soldiers) and one ration per day; $3 of which would be paid in clothing.

Parts of Company A and D were recruited from Calhoun County. Chester J. Murry of Battle Creek was captain of the company and Abner Van Dyke of Marshall was the first lieutenant of Company D. John Henry Jackson (the first African-American child born in Battle Creek) was among the more than 200,000 African Americans who served in the Union Army and Navy.

Sojourner Truth Comes to Battle Creek

The Civil War allowed colored men to take up arms to fight for their freedom. One of those lost in the fight was the grandson of Sojourner Truth. She learned of his death from a letter sent to the grandmother of James Caldwell, who was enlisted in the 54th Regiment along with Truth's grandson. The letter, dated February 25, 1864, stated that Truth's grandson, *"fought bravely at Fort Wagner but he was not found. He must have been taken prisoner or drowned."*

By that time Truth had become well known as an evangelist, and as an advocate for the rights of women. She was born in

1797 in New York as Isabella Baumfree. She had five children with a slave named Thomas. In 1827, she escaped slavery with the assistance of a Quaker family with whom she lived for a year after New York passed its State Emancipation Act.

Truth spoke at the Women's Rights Convention in Akron, Ohio in 1851. Five years later she was invited to speak in Battle Creek, by Quaker Henry Willis. She enjoyed the town and later purchased a home in Harmonia (now called Fort Custer Industrial Park) just west of Battle Creek.

The year her grandson was killed in the war, she visited President Abraham Lincoln. During their meeting he signed her autograph book with the words, "For Aunty, Sojourner Truth. A. Lincoln. Oct. 29, 1864."

At her death, she left her home to her daughter, Sophia, who was an infant at the time of Truth's escape from slavery. Sophia married Thomas Schuyler and later died in poverty on a farm in Marshall, Michigan. Sophia's daughter, Fannie, married a blue-eyed Irishman named Frank Liechuy. As time passed some family members took on their white culture and began to "pass" for white, and for decades, hid their true cultural roots.

After the Civil War, the country was coming into a new era. There was a need for a reprieve from the past, and that reprieve came through music.

Perry Sanford came to Michigan on the Underground
Railroad. He is pictured here with wife, Elvira
~Martich Collection~

Erastus Hussey was key
in the Underground Railroad
efforts in Battle Creek.
~Martich Collection~

Bormay & Co., N.Y.

Well known routes.　Routes not well established ━ ━ ━

**ROUTES THROUGH INDIANA AND MICHIGAN
IN 1848.**

As traced by Lewis Falley

Clockwise: A sketch of Sojourner Truth during the time she made Battle Creek her home in the mid-1800s.

Truth in a painting reflecting one of the meetings she had with President Abraham Lincoln.

A landmark plaque located in Oakhill Cemetery in Battle Creek, Michigan where Truth is buried.

A copy of the autograph presented to Truth by Lincoln six months before his death in 1864.

~Martich Collection~

Mt. Zion A.M.E. Church in Battle Creek was
founded in 1855 by former slaves. The church
pictured was complete in 1906 and is presently
located at 364 West Van Buren Street.
~Martich Collection-Willard Library~

Payton Grayson and his family escaped slavery and came to Battle Creek after meeting Sojourner Truth. He is shown here with the horses he used to start his own business.

~Martich Collection~

Unidentified soldiers visiting with family during WWI at Fort Custer, Battle Creek, MI

~Martich Collection~

Part 2

A Sweet Melody:
The Music Begins

Dance at Hamblin Center around 1945
~Martich Collection~

One is made to wonder how a race subjected to such cruelties could have had the heart to sing at all; much more that they could have sung so sweetly throughout all the dark and dismal night of slavery.

Author Eileen Southern from her book, *Readings in Black Music*.

The city of Battle Creek began to develop and form its own unique identity as the people began to find their own way...and their own voice. In 1865 the federal government attempted to pick itself up after a four-year civil war that had claimed the lives of more than 600,000. The struggle of freed slaves to find their place in the country proved just as challenging.

Some stayed in communities that had seen them as the property of slaveholders for hundreds of years. Others ventured to new areas with only the clothing on their backs. For the first time, all blacks in America were free. The Freedman's Bureau was established by Congress to assist the thousands of former slaves. Many former slaves retreated to Washington D.C., where they sought help from the country's lawmakers. The mission of the Freedman's Bureau was to feed, treat, and shelter the four million freed slaves of the Confederacy.

In 1866, the Civil Rights Act granted blacks the full and equal benefits of all laws. In 1867, the Reconstruction Act forced former Confederate states to ratify a constitution acceptable to Congress. In the meantime, blacks were being elected to Congress, and sharecropping became a way of life for thousands in the South.

That newfound independence for blacks was not tolerated by hate groups such as the Ku Klux Klan. Soon political efforts rescinded the Civil Rights Act, finding it unconstitutional in 1883. Violence against blacks ran rampant, and through 1925 an average of 100 blacks per year were lynched by the Klan or others with similar missions.

Through all the trials and triumphs which came with their newfound freedom, music was an outlet for many blacks, just as the work songs and spirituals had once echoed throughout the plantations. Those who once played music for the guests of the slaveholder were now free to use their talents to entertain themselves. In the book, *Readings in Black Music*, author Eileen Southern, summed up how music served as an escape for blacks who were facing the birth of the Ku Klux Klan and Jim Crow segregation.

She states: "The history of colored people in this country establishes the fact, too, that no system of cruelty, however great or long inflicted, can destroy that sympathy with musical sounds that is born with the soul. Only death itself can end it here on earth while we are taught that for ever and ever Heaven shall be rich in harmony formed by the songs of the redeemed."

By 1870 Battle Creek's population was 5,838, a nearly 74% percent increase in ten years. The black population totaled 315; a more than 100% increase from the previous decade.

In 1884 Frederick Douglass was the keynote speaker at the city's largest Emancipation Day celebration. He was paid $300 for his appearances, and he and his wife were guests in the home of John J. Evans. Evans was a founder of the local black orchestra and was one of the town's most prosperous black citizens. The barbershop owner was instrumental in obtaining quality black bands from all over Michigan to compete at events such as Emancipation Day and perform at local concerts.

The Fisk Jubilee Singers of Fisk University in Tennessee came to the city to perform a repertoire of what was then called, "Plantation Songs." Music typically sung among slaves in their own quarters became a form of entertainment and fundraising for Fisk University. The students traveled across the country and the world, to raise funds to purchase a new site for Fisk University. In the seven years they toured, they sang for everyone from Mark Twain to Queen Victoria. Their efforts brought back $20,000 to the school; the equivalent of millions of dollars today.

The great reviews and responses to their music led them to perform in Battle Creek on several occasions. Many of the black musicians who visited Battle Creek did so through the efforts of various churches with black membership. During the turn of the century, the churches were the foundation for spiritual guidance and fellowship.

A Place of Their Own

Although many blacks had become successful, Jim Crow segregation allowed whites to hold onto feelings of superiority. Some blacks worked in the city's plush Post Tavern (many as waiters), where they could not enjoy its food or other services. And although they were in the North, Jim Crow laws prevented them from entering the front door of their own jobs.

The church was an outlet, a place to worship freely, organize events, and recognize one another in positions of authority. But more was needed. A host of local clubs and organizations become a respite for some. In 1911 the Diamond Club was one of those places. It was located on Madison Street and was "noted for its gambling raids," according to a local newspaper article that quoted members of the Empire Club had been organized to pursue "an educational aspect."

The Colored Protective League and Order of Social Brotherhood hosted events such as the first state convention of Colored Voters of the United States in 1884. For entertainment, there were new sounds of music called the Blues. This music that told stories of love and life through swanky voiced singers who performed in front of the whine of a guitar, or the tinkling of piano keys.

Jazz came right behind the Blues. It was an acceptable music form that could be enjoyed and performed by the city's influential blacks. The Men's Chorus and Colored Cornet Band were popular for their performances at dances and concert events. Vaudeville acts had been a way for black entertainers to make a living after the Civil War. After World War I, music was taking a turn. In 1920 Mamie Smith became the first of her race to be recorded on wax with her song, "Crazy Blues." Smith's success led other blacks to break into the recording business. Blues men such as Sonny Terry, Blind Lemon Jefferson, and Huddie "Leadbelly" Lebetter, all benefitted from this monumental entertainment opportunity.

The popularity of Jazz soon made it to the recording studios and the talents of such greats as Louis Armstrong, recorded with the Hot Five. Small jazz bands eventually expanded to become Big bands. Bands directors like Cab Calloway, Chick

Webb, and Duke Ellington help ignite excitement for large hall concerts. During these high-energy shows, dancers swung their partners in the air, through their legs, and around in circles— never missing a beat.

Until the 1920s there were few places in Battle Creek where a "well respected" black person could go to enjoy entertainment. That soon changed with the forming of two official social clubs in the city known as Soldiers clubs.

The Colored Soldiers Club was located at 41 North McCamly Street. The War Camp Committee Service financed the club for the black soldiers and sailors who were stationed at Fort Custer Military base, which was located on the outskirts of the city. At the club, soldiers could eat at the restaurant which seated up to forty at tables with linen, dishes, and silver. Three pool tables also were available along with a canteen, board games, and magazines.

In 1921 the fine arts added to the creative flair for blacks. The Harlem Renaissance was a cultural movement that included writers such as Langston Hughes, Countee Cullen, and Zora Neale Hurston.

In the music arena, Ma Rainey and Bessie Smith were favorites. After World War I, the popular surge in music led Harry Pace to found the first black-owned record company, Black Swan. Blues singer Ethel Waters was the company's most successful artist and was accompanied on the tour by the company's musical director, Fletcher Henderson and his Black Swan Jazz Masters band. It was this experience that Waters used to help Henderson refine his style.

During this time, Battle Creek musician Clyde Higgins was making his mark in the music world. The jazz saxophone player was born in Shangler, Georgia, and moved to Battle Creek in 1924. During the mid-1920s to early 1940s he traveled with those such as Duke Ellington, Jay McShane, Walter Barnes, and Ray Brown.

Higgins later formed his own band, the Jungle Imps, but he was still sought after by popular orchestras. He joined the Walter Barnes Orchestra. During one of their stops in Memphis, he did not make the performance for some strange reason. That night, a fire engulfed the dance hall where many of the orchestra and club patrons died.

After traveling with other orchestras, Higgins returned to Battle Creek and taught private music lessons in his home. Although he lived outside of the limelight, his talents were admired. Higgins died in 1978 at age of 69. Ray Brown, who once played for the Merv Griffin television show, said Higgins was considered to be the world's greatest alto saxophone player by his contemporaries of the Big Band era of the 1930s.

The good times seemed endless until the Stock Market Crash of 1929. The Crash took the country for a plunge. Banks were unable to give loans to businesses, employers were forced to lay off workers, and spending declined. Many big bands dissolved due to lack of work. By 1932, one-fourth of the nation's workers were jobless. The Battle Creek Sanitarium also would succumb to the financial meltdown. The wealthy clients who once frequented the sanitarium founded by the Kellogg brothers, (W.K. and Dr. John Harvey) no longer could afford the lavish health treatments offered.

The U.S. Government stepped in with A New Deal Agency. The agency created the Works Progress Administration (WPA), which funded a variety of projects to create jobs for all Americans. One of the projects was geared toward artists. Talented artists and musicians gained access to community art schools, art materials, galleries, and opportunities to obtain salaries from the sale of their works. A new era of creation had begun.

Art by Jacob Lawrence, Joseph Delaney, and Raymond Steth depicted the life of everything from slavery and the Civil War, to and everyday moments of life in the black community. Battle Creek artists too joined in on the opportunity to express their creative talents for wages. The city's best musicians performed at dances and organizational events. Some of those popular musicians included Joe Belcher, Odie Thomas, Ted Collins, Troy Slow, Jimmy Steele, Percy Henderson, Bob Burch, and Odie Cromwell. Cromwell had come to Battle Creek in 1919 in flight from the racism in Texas. His stepfather lived in "the bottoms" of Battle Creek (an area where a majority of blacks lived) at a time when the city had a population of more than 30,000; 2,000 of which were black.

Cromwell joined other musicians of the city. Articles in the *Battle Creek Enquirer* state he was considered one of the top ten saxophonists in the world. He told stories of playing with Lester Young in 1926 in New York, and the opportunity to travel to California with Louis Armstrong to take part in the movie, *Sally*.

Although Cromwell didn't take Armstrong up on his offer, he later ventured to California to write and arrange music for Mel Torme. Cromwell later formed his own band, which traveled what he called, the Corn Belt. In 1930 they played at a radio station in South Dakota where they alternated with another group. The leader of the other group was Lawrence Welk, who went on to host his own television show.

Traveling with his family became a strain on them all, so he returned to Battle Creek to settle down. His son, Odie "Jackey" Cromwell recalled musicians coming to their home to visit and play with his father.

"I was young then and didn't know who they were," Jackey said. "I now remember names like Bob Burch (who played drums), Gene Lewis on piano, and Charles Cooper on trumpet."

With the rise of local entertainers, came the need for more adequate places to perform. In 1928 Clifford Marshall provided just that. When his father George died, Clifford decided to quit his job as the head bellman at the Post Tavern hotel to become the first president of his own club, the Bellman's and Waiter's Club.

He partnered with friend, Louis Maxwell, and together they opened the club at 86 Southwest Capital Avenue in the city's downtown. That first year they had 158 members who each paid a $25 a year membership.

The members of the club included bellman, waiters, chauffeurs, cooks, Pullman car porters, soldiers, and other laborers and business owners.

"Before Bellman's and Waiter's, black folks had no place to go where they could get a (alcohol) drink and dance and relax," said Thomas Snyder, who was head bartender at the Athelstan Club for twenty three years. He joined the Bellman and Waiter's Club in the 1940s.

At the Bellman's and Waiter's Club, the after work and weekend respite for blacks featured live music. Because it was located on the I-94 corridor between Chicago and Detroit traveling bands on their way to gigs in the big cities made stops in Battle Creek to perform, or just enjoy the club scene. Members received a special membership card, which allowed them privileged entry after ringing the doorbell to the club's front door.

Nearly ten years after the opening of the Bellman's and Waiter's Club (and four years after the repeal of prohibition), the club was granted a liquor license in 1937. According to the Michigan Liquor Control Commission, this licensing made it the only club in the region where a black person could buy an alcoholic drink, talk politics, and simply fellowship. The club's membership swelled and whites in the city weren't pleased.

In 1941, 700 people signed a petition to the Liquor Control Commission not to reissue the club's liquor license because "inasmuch as the neighborhood was 100% white people and the above-mentioned establishment is operated by colored people. It caters to colored people only."

The petition was denied, and the club continued to thrive.

The African American soldiers stationed at Fort Custer during World War II made up about 90% of the club's membership. Snyder said during the club's height of popularity, boxer Sugar Ray Robinson visited during his military service at Fort Custer.

By the 1950s, the club had more than 500 members. During that year, the city witnessed Jackie Robinson perform at Bailey Stadium with the Brooklyn Dodgers. More than 5,000 turned out for the game to see Robinson. Although he batted only once (singling before going to the sidelines), the fans did get to enjoy the first tastes of Sugar Crisp cereal, which was being promoted at the game by one of the city's cereal giants, Post Cereals.

Battle Creek's affluent patronized the Bellman's, while continuing their roles as leaders in the community. Clifford Marshall was an avid supporter of the local Boy Scouts and provided funds to send boys to scout camp. He served as president of the club until the 1970s when Thomas Snyder became president. Snyder later purchased the club from Clifford.

Snyder remembers the rooms above the club served as lodging for traveling musicians or other African Americans who weren't welcome at many of the city's hotels.

"We had a full house all the time," he said. "In those days there weren't too many places to go. On Sundays we would have matinees (open jam sessions). Bands were a dime a dozen; everybody wanted to become famous."

Snyder said the good time had by traveling Pullman porters and soldiers gave the club a reputation that brought more visitors.

Background, the Battle Creek Sanitarium was a place for the wealthy to come for health and wellness treatments. Top: W.K. Kellogg and his brother, (below) Dr. John Harvey Kellogg created Corn Flakes.*~Martich Collection~*

John "Pat" Patterson was born in 1872, in Omaha, Nebraska. He played for the Columbia Giants of Chicago Negro League team from 1899-1900. He came to Battle Creek in 1901 to play for the Malta Vita company baseball team, however made a name as the city's first Black police officer.

He also led Battle Creek Central High School's baseball team to its first state championship in 1907. Below, Patterson as a policeman, team photo.
~Martich Collection

George Marshall, center, was an established man, well respected in church as a trustee. Insets: left, George and his brother Perry pose as young men; right, Perry would later work at the Bellman's and Waiter's Club purchased by his nephew Clifford Marshall. ~*Martich Collection*~ An original Bellman's and Waiter's Membership card. ~*Sonya Hollins Collection*~

Above, local band with members from left, Ollie Bynam, Percy Henderson, Odie Cromwell, and Johnny Broadanax.

Below, the Men's Chorus: Top from left: Spencer Henderson, Seymour Wilson, Lawrence Harris, William Thompson, Claude Johnson, Charles Strudder, Claude Evans, Perry Marshall;

Bottom from left, Paul Shelton, Sprat Jackson, Robert Scott, Margaret Bradley, Charles Johnson, Clyde Guy, Donnelly Jones.
~Willard Library~

The Bellman's and Waiter's Club was located at 86 Capital Ave. S.W. in Battle Creek. Thomas Snyder, the last owner of the club, is shown serving some of the club's few faithful members.~*Battle Creek Enquirer*~

Dr. Claude Evans became the town's first Black dentist. He graduated from the University of Michigan School of Dentistry in 1917.
~Martich Collection~

The Fisk Jubilee Singers of Nashville's Fisk University performed in Battle Creek on many occasions, often invited by local churches.
~John Hope and Aurelia F. Franklin Library, Fisk University~

The Chicken Car was located on Capital Avenue S.W. and was owned by Ben F. Grayson. The car would serve both blacks and whites.
~Frances Thornton Collection~

The Hamblin Community Center was a place the entire family could enjoy. Its talent shows would be remembered for decades to come. Clockwise from right, Ernie Townsend and friends get an early taste of the spotlight.

The Thatch Children were known for their tap dance routines. Girls joined forces for a high-kickin' chorus line. Ed Joplin played the sax as girls awaited their turn for the stage. Melvin Blackamore and Diane Smith move and groove to the beat.

~Ernie Townsend Collection~

Sy Oliver

Sy Oliver plays trumpet in Jimmie Lunceford Band
~*New York Public Library*~

"It happened one night at Brighton Beach in Brooklyn. I'd given my notice to Jimmie (Lunceford) and Bobby Burns, Tommy (Dorsey's) manager was out there and said, 'Come on in and talk with Tommy.' So he drove me in to the hotel and we went up to Tommy's room. I remember he was shaving, and turned to me and said, 'Sy, whatever you are making playing and writing for Jimmie, I'll pay you $5,000 a year more.' I said, "Sold!" and that was it."

Sy Oliver as interviewed in George Simon's *Big Band.*

Throughout the depression, the music kept toes tappin' in the grandest of nightclubs and creakiest juke joints. Despite the nation's problems, music was a way to provide an escape.

As people begin to have fun again, dance and enjoy life, music developed a new life of its own--Swing. The music led to a dance craze called, the Jitterbug. The dance required plenty of room for legs to swing and men to fling their female partners high in the air, hands tightly locked, only to return her back down and between his legs, and around his neck or waist. Those dancing could truly get into a rhythm with the blare of trumpets and rumble of drums, which were signature to the Big Band Sound.

One of the songs that had dancer's hitting the floor was, "Yes, Indeed." What many in Battle Creek may not have known was that the man responsible for arranging and composing that hot number was one of their own, Melvin James "Sy" Oliver.

Oliver was born in Battle Creek on December 17, 1910, to Melvin and Alice Oliver. His father was a waiter (possibly at the Post Tavern), and his mother a housewife. They left the city and moved to Zanesville, Ohio when Oliver was a young child. His parents were music teachers and active members of their church as choir director and organ players. They wanted him to learn the piano. His interests, however, were in sports. But, his father felt sports would not help his son as he grew older, and was persistent in teaching young Oliver to play the trumpet.

When Oliver was 17 years old, his father died. As the eldest of five children he used his talent as a trumpet player to help his family and got a job with a band led by Zack Whyte.

While in the band he also doubled as a drummer, however, he still dreamed of becoming a lawyer. He constantly read books to keep his mind sharp for the day he hoped to return to school. It was during his time that Whyte gave Oliver a nickname he would keep for life.

The story goes that Whyte asked Oliver why he read so much? Was it that he wanted to become a doctor? Oliver replied jokingly, "Yes, a psychologist" Whyte began calling him, "Sy" for short.

Oliver soon began to arrange compositions for the band. It was during this time his ears perked while listening to the Jimmie Lunceford band rehearsing in Cincinnati. When it came to showmanship, Lunceford's band topped all others. They not only played to tantalize the ear, but they entertained the eye. Oliver wanted to be a part of it.

Their elaborate routines included a synchronized throwing up of the horns in the air, while saxophone players charged off stage in beat, and the trombone section did their own little routine, sliding their horns from left to right. The musicians pretended to outdo the other sections and had laughs and humorous dialog in between.

Oliver wrote several arrangements and presented them to Lunceford. Without hesitation, he was accepted to the band as arranger and musician in 1933. Oliver was so excited to be a part of the band that he composed some of its greatest hits for $2.50 per arrangement. With Oliver's musical genius and their dynamic stage presence, Jimmie's band performed hits that became synonymous with the Big Band era. Songs such as "Stomp it Off," "Dream of You," "Swanee River," "For Dancers Only," "'Tain't Whatcha Do," and "Ain't She Sweet," had dance halls swinging all over the world.

The life was exciting to Oliver, but, as time went on the vigorous tour schedules began to wear on him. It wasn't unusual for the band to perform 200 one-nighters a year. They could easily work in theaters fifteen to twenty weeks out of the year and be in one location four weeks straight. If lucky, they got two weeks of vacation sprinkled somewhere in between traveling more than 40,000 miles a year.

Oliver and other members of the band respected Lunceford. He was a leader who led by example. Because of that, the band members dealt with the long hours of highly intense performances, night after night. Lunceford's strict leadership and tight schedules began to wear thin on Oliver, however, wanted to do more composing and arranging in one place as opposed to juggling this craft with the constant travel schedule.

By this time radio had become the medium for actors and musicians to share their craft with thousands of listeners at once. Colored bands were hardly, if ever, featured on radio programs, unlike their white counterparts who achieved instant success through the airwaves. It was during this time that Lunceford's band began to break racial barriers in music. In New York, Oliver said music was divided into that from above 110th Street, and that below 110th Street—one for Negro audiences, and one for white audiences.

However, once Lunceford's band received regular airplay from the Cotton Club where they performed, colored music became popular across the color line. Despite the success Oliver needed more.

"I'd grown tired of traveling," Oliver said. "I felt I was going out of the world backwards. I wanted to stay in New York and study and write. But (Lunceford) didn't want me to go until he could find another trumpet player to take my place. He kept me in the band until I just quit one night, and then I found out that he had Gerald Wilson waiting in New York all the time, ready to come in as soon as I cut out."

For Tommy Dorsey, Oliver's expertise was just what he needed. In 1935 Dorsey walked off the bandstand of the Glen Island Casino. He was leaving the Dorsey Brothers band, which he led with his brother Jimmy. At the same time, Benny Goodman's orchestra was one of their most fierce competitors, and Tommy would need an arranger just as good as Goodman's Fletcher Henderson. Oliver fit the bill.

For Dorsey's band, Oliver was the arranger and occasional vocalist and trumpet player. He created such hits for the band as, "Easy Does It," "Opus I," "Sunny Side of the Street," and "Yes, Indeed." Hits created by Oliver and other Dorsey composers led him to become known as "The Sentimental Gentleman of Swing."

Oliver was extremely busy in 1943. He led a band while stationed in the Army and was orchestrator on such Hollywood films as, "Dubarry Was a Lady," (1943); "Girl Crazy," (1943); and "Broadway Rhythm" (1944). After his military service,

Oliver left Dorsey's band. In 1946, he created his own band called, *Endorsed by Dorsey*. Oliver merged into what would be his claim to fame. He became musical director for such record labels as Decca, where he arranged music for such vocal greats as Frank Sinatra, Louis Armstrong, Ella Fitzgerald, and Bing Crosby. The Jimmy Lunceford band continued to travel, however, the hectic travel schedule soon caught up with the band leader. Lunceford died of a heart attack in 1947 while on tour.

The birth certificate of Melvin Oliver lists his father as a waiter. His father was most likely employed at the high-class hotel, Post Tavern

Inset, the hotel was built by C.W. Post in 1901, in downtown Battle Creek. Post later was the founder of Post Cereal. *~Frances Thornton Collection~*

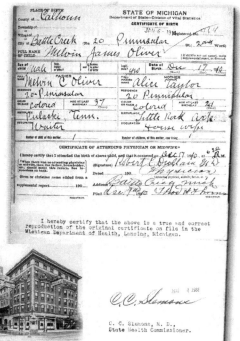

Top, Sy Oliver, right, discusses musical arrangements with singing sensation Frank Sinatra. Bottom left, Oliver conducts a band at the Rainbow Room in New York. Bottom right, Oliver plays trumpet; the instrument that helped him land his first job in a band.

~New York Public Library~

Young Percy Henderson
as an entertainer.

Top, in the late 19th century, Battle Creek's blacks and white citizens worked to help build the community.

Bottom, Battle Creek Central High School Chorus members in 1922 includes Merze Tate (middle row second from the right) who became the first African American graduate of Oxford University.
~Willard Public Library~

Downtown Battle Creek in the early
1900s when Post Tavern dominated the
block. Cutout, John J. Evans, owned
the largest barbershop (below) in Battle
Creek during early 1900s.

~Martich Collection~

. The first wedding held at Hamblin Center USO, Nov 8, 1943, of Ruth
Grant to Woodrow Carr, wedding party L-R

1. Clotie	7. Woodrow Carr	13. Irie Ashley
2. Maxine Johnson	8. Ruth Grant	14. Bert Smith
3. Mary Scott	9. Lois Midgett	15. Rev H Speights
4. Geraldine Ashley	10. Hugh Cheatham	16. Vincent Grant
5. Bernice Cheatham	11. Adell Braxton	
6. Arlene Braxton	12. Williams	

Children in Front L-R

1. Emma Jean Lyons	3. Maxine Lyons
2. Bertha Silverson	4. Connie Bynum

In 1941, the Hamblin
Community Center was
founded as a U.S.O.
Club for black soldiers. It
evolved into a community
center for all ages.

Top, In 1960 the Rev. Dr. Martin Luther King, Jr., spoke at Battle Creek's First United Methodist Church. Bottom, the 43 men and one woman crew of the Kellogg Company Janitor Corp were responsible for keeping the building spotless.

~Martich Collection~

Richard Nixon stopped in Battle Creek in 1968 on his campaign for president against Hubert Humphrey.
Below: Opposers to Nixon picket.
~Battle Creek Enquirer~

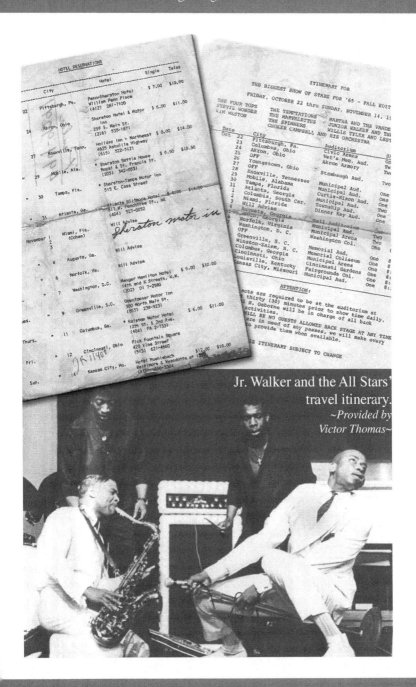

Jr. Walker and the All Stars'
travel itinerary.
~*Provided by*
Victor Thomas~

In 2009, Blues singer Lou Wilson was honored during a musical tribute in Battle Creek. His musical career began as a youngster. The Fabulous Newcomers included Wilson, seated; and Ed Hosley, James Kelley and Lewis Glade.

~Photos provided by James Kelley and Sonya Bernard-Hollins~

Top, Jazz drummer, Bill Dowdy performed with Blue Note Records' *The Three Sounds*.

Left, musician Jim Cummings was inspired by local artists at the El Grotto to form his own band. Today he owns Soundstage 1 in Climax, MI.

"I would be the only white person in the club; watching and learning. What I learned there helped me in my career, even today."
Jim Cummings

Top, Bobby Holley performs in military and later makes the charts. He is honored with Helen Montgomery Award in 2003 by Sonya Hollins. Bottom right, Melvin Blackamore performs.

Base player Bobby Parker owned a small jazz club in downtown Battle Creek where he and other musicians held weekly jam sessions for decades.

Below, Battle Creek natives and performers Nicolas and Jeremy Holder pose with Shamar Moore, backstage at an event in Los Angeles, California (2002).

𝒫𝒶𝓇𝓉 3
Here I Stand: The Do Wop

Battle Creek Central Follies- 1956
~Ernie Townsend Collection~
Pictured from left: Joyce Jones, Erma (Lyons) Horsley,
Odessa (Marshall) Dawson, Faye Askew

"We had dreams, we had goals. We helped each other
because we knew when we hit the stage, we
had to come correct."
Bobby "The Entertainer" Holley

Making a Way

In 1930 there were more than 43,500 people in Battle Creek; nearly 2,000 were black. While the population was growing, the roots planted by early leaders in the city began to see opportunities open to blacks.

They opened businesses, which provided stability and some wealth for their families. Daniel Patton Sr. became the first black resident in the city to open a funeral service. A native of Nashville, Tennessee, he and his wife Miggie, (Crawford) first operated their business out of 103 Warren Street. It later moved to 407 West Van Buren Street, and finally to 116 Main Street where they lived next door. In 1933 Benjamin Franklin Eason opened the Blue Moon Café, famous for his sweet potato pies and beef stew. He leased the space at 172 McCamly Street. In 1938 he became night janitor at City Hall.

Local businessman Silas Thompson also owned a restaurant tavern business at South Kendall and Hamblin Avenue called the Black and Tan. It opened in 1936 as a gathering place for both blacks and whites. During World War II, the clientele became mostly soldiers stationed at Fort Custer Military Base just outside of town. Many attended the Black and Tan for dinner, or after theater shows at the Post Theatre. The club became one of the many properties Thompson would own in town.

The hard work of black business owners, particularly those in the restaurant business, was a major benefit to their children. Fred Moore bought a streetcar which he converted into a restaurant and positioned it on Capital Avenue S.W. His menu contained such specials as chicken, soup, and sandwiches. His son Amos worked with the family, in addition to being a carrier for the *Enquirer and News* where he was named Best Carrier in 1923.

Amos graduated from Battle Creek Central High School in 1925 and moved to Chicago to attend a trade school for commercial printing. That skill led him to Philadelphia where he would eventually work for Krosof Brothers Printing Company. He also operated a greeting card business from his home and helped organize the first Black Business directory in Philadelphia.

His father's streetcar was sold to Benjamin Franklin (B.F.) Grayson who continued to operate the business as Chicken Charlie's for thirty years; catering to both black and white customers. In 1919 customers at Chicken Charlie's could get hot steaks for 25 cents, pork chops for 35 cents, eggs and ham or eggs and bacon for 30 cents, and an ice cold pop for 5 cents.

Ben's father Payton, had roots in the city. A young Payton was with his parents and siblings who had just escaped slavery in Virginia when they met Sojourner Truth in Freedman's Village just outside Washington D.C. It is believed that it was Truth who convinced the family to come to Battle Creek when she met them during her trip to D.C. to meet President Lincoln.

Music, Dance, and a Good Time

In 1941 the United Service Organization clubs (USO) opened a location on South Kendall in Battle Creek for black soldiers who were serving at Fort Custer during War World II. The club brought new opportunities to entertain.

The Bellman's and Waiter's Club thrived and other clubs came along to share in their success. Clubs such as the Fleetwood, Vista, and Elks opened. Some adopted the membership-only motto. However, the opening of the USO club brought on a new energy. While it did its part to entertain the colored soldier, it would emerge into something more.

In 1947, when entertaining the troops had faded with the end of World War II, a new era was beginning. The USO became the Hamblin Community Center. Many of those who would later have a thirst for the life of an entertainer, began this dream at the Hamblin Community Center's talent shows.

Julia Milner became the director of the center and created a place where (mostly black) children came to enjoy everything from organized sports to etiquette classes. It was a home away from home and a place to gather with friends. Adults too utilized the building for organization meetings, social gatherings, and wedding receptions.

However, one of the most popular happenings at the Hamblin Community Center was its talent shows. Children and adults brought their best acts to the stage to find out if they could get the standing-room only crowds to use their applause to vote them as the audience favorite.

"It was something everybody looked forward to, I mean everybody, young and old," said Ernie Townsend, a native of the Battle Creek and former Hamblin talent show performer.

"You could have a son playing an instrument, and then his father comes on next, singing; it was literally, for many, a family affair."

Townsend said those who performed did so in the sense of entertainment and unity. Musicians performed with their own bands, and in the next act, they would be playing back-up for a vocalist. Girls formed quartets and wore frilly dresses, and a few acts later appeared in shorts and sneakers to join in more than a dozen girls in a chorus line number.

For decades the Hamblin Community Center in Battle Creek served the African American population's entertainment needs.
~Sonya Hollins Collection~

The El Grotto Lounge

The foundation of entertainment set by the Hamblin Community Center was just enough to help fuel the beginnings of The El Grotto Lounge. The showmanship and spirit of competition carried over into a new venue by those whose roots began at the center's talent shows.

The club was founded by husband and wife team, Robert "Snap", and Helen Montgomery. Robert moved to Battle Creek from Culp, Illinois in 1926. He later worked at the Kellogg's cereal factory and served in the U.S. Navy during World War II. One night, when he went out for a drink at a local tavern, he paid the bartender and began to leave. Suddenly he hear a glass break. It had been his glass; a glass the white bartender refused to wash and reuse for their white customers. That infuriated Snap. He went home to his wife and told her what happened. What could they do about it?

The couple took a chance, quit their jobs, and opened a club in 1949. They called it "The Corner," as it was located on the corner of Kendall and Hamblin streets on the city's Westside. The bar served wine and beer and did not require membership to enter. It soon expanded from the corner, next door to 44 South Kendall Street, where a pool hall had recently closed. The name of the club changed after a visit to California.

"(They) visited California, and heard the name El Grotto somewhere," said Melvin Evans. "They liked the name, and change the club to The El Grotto Lounge."

Left, Helen Montgomery was owner of the El Grotto Lounge for decades. Her inspiration led many musicians to aim for the big stage.

Middle, Melvin Evans, Helen's brother.

Bottom, Robert "Snap" Montgomery, and wife, Helen, visit with her brother and sister-in-law in California where they heard the name, El Grotto.

~Photo provided by Melvin Evans collection~

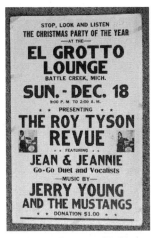

STOP, LOOK AND LISTEN
THE CHRISTMAS PARTY OF THE YEAR
—AT THE—
EL GROTTO LOUNGE
BATTLE CREEK, MICH.
SUN. - DEC. 18
9:00 P. M. TO 2:00 A. M.
* * PRESENTING * *
THE ROY TYSON REVUE
* * FEATURING * *
JEAN & JEANNIE
Go-Go Duet and Vocalists
—MUSIC BY—
JERRY YOUNG AND THE MUSTANGS
* * DONATION $1.00 * *

~Poster: Courtesy of Bobby Holley.~

Jackey & Johnny

Jackey Beavers and Johnny Bristol were Motown artist who helped bring along other acts from Battle Creek to Detroit's Hitsville U.S.A. *~Velma Adams Collection*

Jackey & Johnny

In the club's early days, many came for the music played by jukebox, and a place to enjoy beer and wine with their friends. But, the arrival of two Fort Custer soldiers changed the course of the club forever. Those soldiers were Robert "Jackey" Beavers and Johnny Bristol. The two met in 1956 in the barracks at Selfridge Air Force Base near Mount Clemens, Michigan. Beavers was in the shower when he heard Bristol and another soldier singing. Beavers recalled joining in.

"I was humming when (Bristol) said, 'You sang?' I said, "Yeah, I sang," Beavers recalled.

The Cartersville, Georgia native was asked by Bristol (from Morgantown North Carolina) to, "hit this (tune)." Bristol liked what he heard and decided to form a group. He, along with Beavers and three others, became *The Five Jokers.*

After much practice, the group finally landed an opportunity to perform at Detroit's Twenty Grand Club. The club opened in 1953 by Leo and Kabbush and located along Warren Avenue. The club owners sought entertainment for its exclusively high-class black clientele and offered an opportunity for black musicians to perform and enjoy their music in style. In 1958 the club was destroyed after a fire. However, it was rebuilt with an even more lavish appeal and included a bowling alley on the first level, and the Gold Room to enjoy performances.

The debut of *The Five Jokers* was a success. They were invited back for the weekend show. Before the gig, three members of the group changed their minds about performing. Beavers and Bristol refused to give up the opportunity to perform in one of the most popular clubs in Michigan. They voted to drop the other members and became a duo. From now on, they would be known as *Jackey and Johnny.*

Together they won talent shows both on and off the military base. Their reputation preceded them and soon were introduced to a young woman named Gwendolyn Gordy. Gwendolyn quickly became their manager, and six months later the duo began recording on Anna Records, and Harvey Fuqua's Tri-Phi label. Anna, Gwendolyn's sister, held a label under the umbrella of their brother's company, Hitsville U.S.A., later known as Motown.

Jackey and Johnny learned a lot about the Gordy family and how they worked together to create a prosperous musical dynasty. Esther Gordy started the family savings club that allowed family members to deposit into and borrow. Brother Berry approached the family for a loan to produce his first record. The family approved him for an $800 loan.

In 1959 he used the money to purchase a two-story home at 2648 West Grand Boulevard in Detroit. He called it, Hitsville U.S.A. That home/recording studio became a place where timeless hits were recorded on such labels, (named after family members), as Tamla, Anna, Soul, MoWest and family name, Gordy. The Tri-Phi label, lead by Harvey Fuqua, later merged with the Motown label.

Berry used the strategy of various labels to disguise their releases as songs from different record companies, in hopes radio

radio stations would grant more airplay for multiple releases. Gordy's song, "Money (That's What I Want)" was performed by Barrett Strong on the Anna label in 1959. It enjoyed great first-time success and led the way for more triumphs.

Jackey and Johnny had their cake and ate it too. They performed with the label in the evenings and weekends while they fulfilled their military obligations during the day. But, as they began to ride on good times, they both were given orders to transfer to Fort Custer in Battle Creek.

"We went to see the commanding officer–everyone who we thought could get us out of the move. But it didn't work," Beavers said.

The two had no choice but to pack up and reluctantly drive to their new base in Battle Creek, nearly 150 miles from Hitsville U.S.A. As they drove to their new base in Bristol's 1951 Ford, spirits were low. To make matters worse, they arrived into Battle Creek in the midst of a winter blizzard.

On their first Saturday night in town, the soldiers went out with other soldiers to the El Grotto Lounge. They were warned that it was no, Twenty Grand. It was even given the nickname, the "Bucket of Blood," due to the often crowd-dispersing fights. A café was next door to the club and a gas station and other homes surrounded it. Wanting to make the best out of their situation, the duo approached club owner Helen Montgomery about possibly performing at the club.

There had never been live acts at the club, just jukebox music and dancing to accompany the drinking and social atmosphere. Once Helen learned of their Hitsville connection she couldn't refuse. She offered to pay them $25 each night they performed.

"That $25 paid my way out of doing KP (kitchen duty) for a whole year," Beavers said. It wasn't the Twenty Grand club, and it may have been called the Bucket of Blood, but it was heaven to us. After we became a hit at the club, Helen instituted a cover charge for the first time at the club for Friday, Saturday, Sunday, and Monday performances."

The duo began to make the most of their move to Battle Creek and used the El Grotto to hone their skills. At the same time, they traveled up the two-lane road to Motown studios in Detroit at least twice a week where they received artist development classes. They learned etiquette from Maxine Powell, choreography by Cholly Atkins, and voice lessons from Maurice King. Gordy's method of preparing the artists for first-class entertainment would set his performers above those from other record companies.

In 1960 the hard work paid off with the release of their single, "Lonely and Blue." It topped the local charts at No. 4 in Bakersfield, California, then rocketed to No.1. Motown became the first record company to host a tour exclusively of their own artists. Jackey and Johnny wanted to be a part of that. It had been their dream since performing at the Twenty Grand. While they were climbing the record charts, the military couldn't care less about their success with Motown.

They were soldiers first, and still had service to fulfill to the government. Regardless of any pleading or arrangements they attempted to make, the military refused to grant them leave time to perform. Six months prior to their release from duty, their one single had lost all momentum on the charts, and they were no prime candidates for the traveling cadre.

They had missed out on opportunities to perform around the country, but the two were celebrity performers for the local El Grotto and Bellman's and Waiter's clubs. Their performances were so popular they decided to make Battle Creek their home. In addition, they had met and married women from the area and were starting families. Beavers' wife Gloria was from Marshall, and Bristol's wife, Maude, was from Battle Creek.

Beavers found a job at Fort Custer State Hospital and traveled with Bristol to performances on the weekends. After one performance, Beavers missed his plane and arrived at work late to work on that Monday. He was warned by his commander that one more late arrival would be his last.

With a child on the way and a wife to care for, Beavers made a decision that would forever strain his friendship with Bristol for years to come. When the two were scheduled to perform at the Royal Peach in Atlanta, Georgia, Beavers told his friend, he could not go.

"I could either be a star and lose my job, or not go and have a job to take care of my family," Beavers said.

He chose the latter.

"I was miserable, and Johnny was too," Beavers remembered. "Everyone was mad and I don't blame them. I was messing up his career."

After five years of performing together, the two went their separate ways. In 1968 Beavers formed a new band of local musicians, which traveled around Michigan. By this time, Bristol moved closer to Motown where he was a producer for the company. He eventually married Berry Gordy's niece, Iris.

During one Christmas visit back to Battle Creek, the duo put the past behind them as they contemplated a reunion. They wrote the song, "Someday We'll Be Together," and eagerly presented it to Barry. While he liked the tune, he wanted to sign them to a seven-year contract. Beavers, not wanting to be bound to the music industry, declined.

Berry did, however, have another suggestion. Motown's number-one act was about to split up, and he suggested the two forward the song to them–Diana Ross and the Supremes. Ross was making a move toward being a solo career, and the song would allow the Supremes to take their bow from the public eye in style, according to Beavers.

With added producing assistance from Harvey Fuqua (former leader of Harvey and the Moonglows and Motown producer) they produced the song for the Supremes. Shortly after it was released, it topped the charts, earning the girls two gold records in six weeks. The song gave the Supremes their twelfth and last number-one hit.

"I remember going to Las Vegas to see Diana perform," said Beavers. "She invited Johnny and I to sing with her. It was good times."

Posing for Sean Hollins at the Motown reunion event held at the Roostertail in Detroit, MI, (2002)—Johnny Bristol, left, Winnie Brown (former Motown hair stylist), Betty Kelly, (originally a *Velvelette* before becoming one of the *Vandellas*), and member of *The Miracles*, Bobby Rogers.

Above left, during one of his last trips to Battle Creek (1995), Sonya Hollins snaps this photo of Bishop Jackey Beavers and Victor Thomas (former organ player for *Junior Walker and the All Stars*) as Beavers discussed a new initiative created to help released prisoners.

Above right, one of the last gospel CDs recorded by Bishop Jackey Beavers before his death in 2008.

Wade Flemons

Wade Flemons was still a student at
Battle Creek Central High School
when his hit, "Here I Stand," made
him a star in 1958.
~*Velma Adams Collection*~

Jackey and Johnny's position at Motown became infectious. Everybody wanted to perform at the El Grotto in hopes that the Motown artist could put in a good word for them at Motown, or any other label for that matter. Performers came from as far as Chicago to take a shot at perfecting their craft and being discovered. Celebrities who visited the area, often stopped at the El Grotto for good entertainment.

"I remember Muhammad Ali coming here during the time he refused to go to the Army," said Melvin Evans, the club's former bartender. "Leon Spinks even came here. How they would hear about the club, I don't know."

What everyone did know was that there was great entertainment to be found at the El Grotto. One local group wore the glow of star dust around them. They called themselves, *The Shifters*. The standout of the group was Wade Flemons.

Flemons was born in 1940 in Coffeyville, Kansas to Samuel and Kathyrine Flemons. His father was a minister who raised his son in the church where he began to gravitate toward music. He attended third grade at Will Rogers School in Wichita where he joined his first singing group.

He and other elementary school students formed a young gospel group that performed spirituals in the school classrooms. As he grew older, he continued being part of groups that traveled to churches to perform. His love for singing was enhanced as he began to play instruments. In seventh grade, he began to learn to read music and play the viola. In 1955 he moved to Battle Creek to live with his mother and attended Southeastern Junior High School. He instantly became known for his singing and participated in school follies. It was during one of those school follies that he met Jeanette "Nippy" (Holley) Broadway. She attended W.K. Kellogg Junior High School and had only heard of Flemons through a mutual friend, Beverly Olds.

"I had a shy streak in me," Broadway said. "I didn't think he was cute, but he did have a sweet side to him that made him have a little cuteness about him."

The two began seeing one another more often. At the same time, his talent led him to merge with other local guys who formed Do Wop wanna-be groups. He joined one called *The Diamond Aces*.

In 1955 Lou Wilson organized a group called, *The Vandalist*. He then formed a group called, *The Shifters* (which later became *Jesse Blackford and the Diamond Aces*). Again, he reorganized the group and added Flemons, James Kelley, Ed Horsley, Lewis Glade, and himself. They harmonized on street corners in the Washington Heights area every chance they got.

By this time, Flemons was attending Battle Creek Central High School where he sang in the school's A Cappella Choir. He also learned to play piano by ear. Nippy's brother Buddy, played piano, and everyone who had a group wanted Buddy to play for them. His natural talent allowed him to play any type of music, from Spiritual to Jazz.

Buddy along with his two other brothers, Otis "Sonny," Bobby, and two sisters, all lived with their father, the Rev. Otis Holley Sr., who was a local pastor. Their mother also lived in town but had remarried. The Rev. Holley welcomed anyone in the neighborhood to practice at his home as long as they were respectful. They always were. With a piano and plenty of practice time, the group perfected their harmony. They took their act from the street corners to Hamblin Community Center's talent shows.

"They far surpassed any local talent." Broadway said. "They were polished. Their look was professional and they all were good singers," said Broadway who is a member of the singing group, *Nature's Product*. Members of her group include Mike Nunnally, Ernie Townsend and Stanley Tuggle.

She remembers the crowd's reaction once *The Shifters* took stage. When group was announced, the crowd roared in applause and eager anticipation. They wondered if they could be as popular outside Battle Creek and made plans to take their act to another level.

In 1958 Flemons, the songwriter of the group wrote "Here I Stand." He was still in high school. They traveled to Kalamazoo, just twenty minutes down the road, and created a demo at a recording studio. The demo was mailed to various record companies. The guys waited to see it they would get a call for an audition.

One studio reached out and invited them for an audition. That company was Chicago-based Vee Jay Records. Vee Jay was owned by husband and wife team James and Vivian Bracken, and partner Calvin Carter. It was the first large independent record company owned by African Americans, and before Motown was the most successful.

The company was formed in 1953 while Vivian was still a disc jockey at WGRY in Gary, Indiana. Her brother, Calvin, brought his experience as a consultant for Chess Records. The company produced songs in such genres as Blues, Jazz, Do Wop, and Rock & Roll. The company managed such artists as the *Spaniels, El Dorados, Magnificents*, and *Jimmy Reed.* Their Gospel music artists included the popular *Staple Singers,* the *Original Five Blind Boys,* and the *Caravans.* The company made history when they introduced the Beatles to the United States. Hit makers such as Jerry "Iceman" Butler, and Curtis Mayfield and the Dells also called the company home.

Knowing the company's talent pool, *The Shifters* were excited for the opportunity to audition. In July of 1958 a month after cutting their demo, the group was signed to Vee Jay. The friends were excited about their newly found fame...that was until they saw the record cover. They were surprised to see that the group was renamed, *Wade Flemons and the Newcomers.* To top it off, *The Newcomers'* name was twice as small as Flemons.' He was made the star of the group just as *Jerry Butler of The Impressions,* and *Dee Clark* of the *Kool Gents* were singled out in their groups.

The lead singers took center stage while the other members (all good friends) were pushed into the background. Flemons toured the eastern circuit with *The Newcomers*, however, they would eventually be pushed out of sight altogether. Flemons became a solo artist. He appeared on *Dick Clark's American Bandstand* in Philadelphia, *The Alan Freed Show* in New York, *The Buddy Deane Show* in Baltimore, and *The Milt Grant Show* in Washington D.C. "Here I Stand" went to No. 19 on the Billboard R&B chart, and No. 80 on the Pop chart.

In 1960 (in between working with other artists of the label), Flemons recorded "What's Happening," which went to No. 33 on Cash Box R&B chart and No. 94 on Billboard Pop chart. He later eased back to the top of the charts with a remake of a Percy Mayfield song, "Please Send Me Someone To Love." That song made it to No. 20 on the Billboard's R&B chart.

His song, "I Knew You When," written by Joe South, fizzled when he recorded it. However, when it was re-recorded by a white artist, Billy Joe Royal, it hit high on the charts a year after Flemons' recording of the same tune.

"That was the biggest blow he had in his life," said Broadway, who by this time had been engaged to Flemons. Together they had a son, Brian.

Flemons was bound by contract to Vee Jay, which began concentrating on their other artists. In 1965 he cowrote "Stay in My Corner," with Barrett Strong and Eugene Miller for the *Dells*, which reached No. 30 on the R&B charts. With his career at a stand still, he joined the military. At that same time, Vee Jay Records was experiencing a financial blow. Their top performers, *The Four Seasons*, left after contract disputes in 1963. Capital Records took advantage of their option with the company to purchase one of *The Beatles'* songs, "I Want to Hold Your Hand," and by 1967 the company went bankrupt.

Flemons on his own. By then he had befriended other artists on the label. He and Jerry Butler were so close that Flemons was best man in Butler's wedding, and Butler was named Flemons' son Brian's godfather. Butler understood some of the same issues Flemons faced coming into the company.

Butler had been with the Impressions when he too, was brought out as the lead of his group before ill feelings led to their career break up.

"Wade was a genius when it came to writing music," Butler said. "We could be in the car and he would just be concentrating. Next thing we know, he'd say, 'listen to this.' It would be good."

After leaving the military Flemons made another attempt into the music business. While performing in Chicago he met Maurice White who was a Chess Records artist and a member of the Ramsey Lewis Trio. White grew up loving music and played the drums in his school band prior to coming to Chess. He used what he learned from his experiences with Chess and Lewis,' Trio, to take a chance and form his own band. In 1969 he met Flemons near Chess Records on Michigan Avenue where musicians hung out.

Their creative juices began to flow and they decided to form a company to produce jingles for commercials. They rented space at 1321 Michigan Avenue (not far from Chess Records) on what was known as Record Row. They did what they loved; wrote music. Together they created jingles for Budweiser, songs for Flemons to sing, and one for Donnie Hathaway. However, nothing substantial materialize from those efforts.

The two formed their own group and called themselves, *The Salty Peppers*. The group's regional hit, "La, La Time," gave them the courage to moved to California. Their confidence paid off as they soon signed to Capital Records under their new name, *Earth, Wind and Fire*. Sherry Scott and Donald Whitehead were also members of the group. White said they didn't get rich by signing with Capital, and they worked longer than the money stretched.

"We worked from noon to 6 p.m. every day; playing all kinds of music," White said. "We wrote all our own music. We had started as a jazz band and changed our style a bit. In Chicago people were into the Black Power movement, so we wore Dashikis and Afros which were popular then.

"I played drums on everything in the beginning. I was scared to go and sing," White said. "Musically, we were a jazz band and Wade did all the leads on the songs, and that was fine. I remember, on stage, how dynamic he was. I used to call him The Preacher because of his church-like singing style. We loved it. It was great. He came alive on stage."

White said Flemons' energy was contagious and motivated him to hit center stage, to sing.

"Some of (Wade) rubbed off on me. When the time came for me to get out front, I loved it. You couldn't get me back (to drums) after that."

Flemons, along with White and Donald Whitehead, created such songs as "Help Somebody," "Moment of Truth," "Love is Life," and "Fan the Fire." Despite their valiant efforts, their self-titled album entered the Billboard album chart peaking at No. 172. White began to take a lead role which led to ill feelings. Flemons, Scott, and Whitehead left the group.

Top, Wade is performing with Sherry Scott, and Maurice White in their early stages of becoming Earth, Wind and Fire.

~Courtesy of Brian Flemons ~

Bottom left, Wade performed in Battle Creek in 1960 with his hit, "Here I Stand." *~Courtesy of Bobby Holley~* Bottom right, Wade's album cover. *~Rhino Records~*

Royalaiers

The success of their friends inspired Wille Bell, Ernie Townsend, Mike Nunnally, Willie English, and Stanley Tuggle to try their hand at fame under various names such as The Blenders, The Del-Raves, and finally, The Royalaires. ~*Courtesy of Ernie Townsend* ~

With the success of Wade Flemons, other students of Battle Creek Central High School felt they could 'make it' in the music industry. In 1958 (the same year Flemons' hit, "Here I Stand," was released) friends Willie Bell, Ernie Townsend, Mike Nunnally, and Willie English formed a group. After returning from the military, friend Stanley Tuggle joined.

Throughout the years, the group's names and some of the players change. They went from being *The Ravens* one day to *The Del-Raves* the next. They were still in high school and too young to perform at the El Grotto, so they traveled to Grand Rapids as featured artists on a television station dance show. They earned $20 per person after each show and loved it.

The trek toward fame continued as they graduated high school in 1961. They changed their name to *The Blenders* and specialized in four to five-part harmony. In 1964 they created a mass revue of singers, musicians, and dancers (men and women) to perform on a USO Tour. However, once some of the members found out where they would be traveling, all the women, and most of the men dropped out.

"We were hired to perform, not in Germany, Italy, nothing like that," Townsend remembered. "They sent us to Greenland, and other small bases in remote areas where the soldiers rarely got out of field duty!"

Townsend said once soldiers were over the shock that there weren't any women performing with them, they warmed up to their act. However, their last stop sent even him packing for home. Townsend remembers the crowd of soldiers being cold and unappreciative of their performance. That reception, and the fact that they were performing for segregated officers clubs, led them to take the next plane home.

Once back in Battle Creek the group joined former Motown singer Jackey Beavers in a session at Chess Records in Chicago. Beavers invited them to be a part of a song he wanted to create as a spin-off to Junior Walker's "Shotgun." The song was entitled, "Slingshot." On the first day of the session, Tuggle's brand new Impala was stolen right in front of the building.

The group tried their hand at a Motown Records contract. After an audition, they were given a contract and asked to sign immediately. When they didn't, that ended any chances would ever have with that company.

"We didn't want to get stuck with a company who would just 'sit' on our contract. So we left," Tuggle remembers.

The group continued to perform together for years under their final name change to *Nature's Product,* which now included Jeanette "Nippy" Broadway. As each group continued to make their way down the road toward fame together, the theme of "fame breaks up friendships," continued.

The Fayatons consisted of first tenor IV Simpson, high tenor, and piano player Otis "Sonny" Holley Jr., second tenor and bass Walter Garrett, and Melvin "Lamel" Blackamore. They were popular on the local music scene. Some of them had been a part of other bands throughout the years and their reputations preceded them. Blackamore, who moved to Battle Creek from Mounds, Illinois in 1948, admired the style of James Brown and imitated Brown's captivating moves.

The group auditioned for Tri-Fi Records in 1956–the same

label that first signed Jackey and Johnny under the Motown umbrella. That Battle Creek connection paid off and they too received a contract. The group recorded, "Let This Girl," and "Quiet One." After contractual difficulties however, the group left the company, split up, and Blackamore went solo.

With the help of his father, Blackamore was given connections into the 63rd Street club circuit in Chicago where he performed the Blues. He opened for such headlining guests as B.B. King and Battle Creek's own Wade Flemons who was living in the limelight of Vee Jay Records.

"I sort of got the big head," said Blackamore. "It's something when you can get hundreds of people in the palm of your hands and everything goes. It's power. If you don't know how to handle that power, you're fighting a losing game."

He fought that game and learned a hard lesson. For more than two years he had been a popular addition to club line-ups, but had gotten in one too many arguments with the club managers. He was barred from performing in any of the clubs again.

"I thought, if people found out I wasn't performing there anymore, they ain't comin' either," Blackamore said. "But that didn't happen. I went down, down, down, and came back to Battle Creek from a good run in Chicago."

In 1958 he performed locally at the El Grotto, where he was also part of a comedy routine with Jim Sweet, a local promoter. He continued to perform some classic Do Wop tunes, and became known locally as the "Oldies but Goodies Man."

The other members of the Fayatons, IV Simpson, Walter

Garrett, and Sonny Holley continued their careers.

Simpson performed with other local groups, wrote, and produced his own material. Garrett joined in with local groups when needed. But, Sonny Holley had one more chance to become a part of Motown.

Bottom right, The Fayatons from left, IV Simpson, Walter Garrett, Sonny Holley, and Melvin Blackamore.
Bottom left, IV Simpson performs at the El Grotto with house band, Junior Walker and the All Stars.
Headshot, Melvin Blackamore
~Courtesy of Ernie Townsend~

The Blenders 1964

Noted here as *The Blenders,* these friends performed together for decades under various names on their quest for fame. Many of them traveled together to Europe on an eye-opening USO tour.

~*Courtesy of Ernie Townsend* ~

Junior Walker and the All Stars

The house band for the El Grotto Lounge in Battle Creek, Michigan, became Motown Records recording artists who had a hit single, "Shotgun," an iconic hit. Junior Walker (center) poses as (standing from left) Sonny Holley and Willie Woods have his back, and (kneeling) Tony Washington and Jerome Teasley "cover" their leader.

~Courtesy of Sonny Holley ~

With the connection to Motown through Jackey and Johnny, a local house band at the El Grotto Lounge sought to be the next in line for a chance at fame. Autry DeWalt Mixon was born in Blytheville, Arkansas in 1942. The story is, that he loved walking to school instead of taking the bus, so he was nicknamed Junior Walker. The name stuck.

He and his family moved north to South Bend, Indiana where, like many other blacks from the South, they sought the promise of better-paying jobs and a more tolerable racial climate. At age 14, Junior attempted to break into the music business by performing at clubs in Chicago. He hoped to sneak into a nightclub, catch a set with a jazz band, and be discovered. There was only one thing stopping him...the security at the door.

"I would try to sneak in by saying, "Illinois Jacquet is my uncle," Junior said in a 1992 *Battle Creek Enquirer* interview. "They would throw me out. Once I said, 'I am the janitor here to clean up,' and they said, 'Then go clean the street!'"

Junior gave up his attempts and went on to attend high school in South Bend. He met Willie Woods who had recently moved to the city from Morehouse Parish, Louisiana. Woods, born in 1936, had been raised on a farm where his family worked as sharecroppers.

During Woods' childhood, he suffered the degradation of segregation, and even witnessed the hanging of his uncle hanged. While working in the fields with his family, crop dusters often sprayed the crops while they worked in them.

His mother and stepfather moved to South Bend when he

was eight years old where he met other boys who liked to play typical kids games and had a love for music.

Woods and Junior lived less than two blocks apart and shared musical interests. The teens soon met William Nicks, known as Billy "Sticks" Nicks because of his love for the drums. Nicks, a self-taught drummer, became leader of his own band, *The Rhythm Rockers*. In 1956 the band already was a local favorite. Nicks invited Junior's talent as a tenor saxophone player in the group to give it a unique sound. Fred Patton played piano and performed vocals, and Woods came on board to play the guitar.

The Rhythm Rockers performed at local dances throughout South Bend. They became regulars on the local WNDU television station's Club "46" Saturday afternoon dance show for high school students. The group was on its way toward success when disenchantment struck among the members.

Junior left the band and took Woods and Patton with him. Tony Washington would become his drummer. They were now known as *Junior Walker and the All Stars* and began to hit the club scene in South Bend as well as Michigan clubs in Benton Harbor, Albion, Jackson, and Battle Creek.

It was typical for them to play Friday, Saturday, and Sunday in Battle Creek, and later head over to Albion to perform at a breakfast dance (after hours club) until 4 a.m.

On Tuesdays and Thursdays they performed at the East End club in Benton Harbor and drove back home to South Bend after each gig. It took $5 to fill up Junior's Studebaker, and they all pitched in to cover the cost from their divided earnings of up

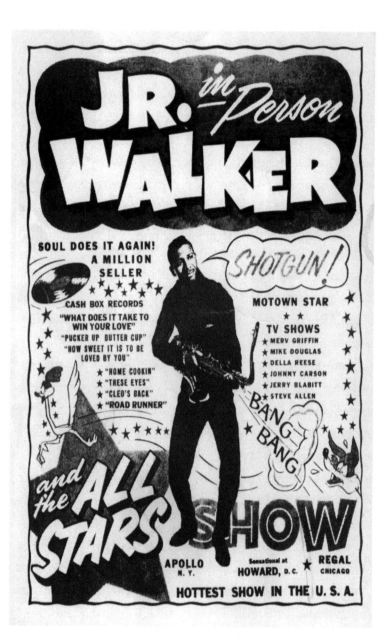

to $20 each a night.

One evening, while driving the back roads from South Bend through Michigan towns Cassopolis, Three Rivers, and Kalamazoo toward Battle Creek, something happened. The car made an unusual noise, and suddenly the springs broke in the car when Junior turned the corner. The friends bounced along to a stop, toppling onto one another. No other cars were on the road, and once they sat there for a few seconds reflecting on what had happened, they all began to laugh.

All they could do was find a pay phone to call Helen Montgomery, owner of the El Grotto Lounge where they were scheduled to play. They told her about their delay and she decided to help them. She sent her brother Melvin, also the club's bartender, to pick them up. Once they arrived, Helen and husband, Snap had good news for them.

The couple offered to purchase a new Buick for Junior to transport his group, but on one condition. They would come to work as her regular house band. They all agreed. They rented apartments, and the club owners later helped Junior purchase a home on Green Street.

After serving in the military, childhood friend Victor Thomas joined the band to replace Fred Patton as the new organ player, and moved from South Bend to Battle Creek.

The band became popular, and fellow El Grotto Lounge performers Bristol and Beavers helped them get an audition with Hitsville's Tri-Phi Records. Their first hit recording was "Cleo's Mood." However, it would be nearly four years before they were back in the studios to record another hit.

In the meantime, *The All Stars* continued as house band and headliners of the El Grotto Lounge; each earning $20 a night. To them, there was nothing better than having fun playing their music and entertaining others. Their interaction with the crowd was something the audience loved. It was this chemistry that member Victor Thomas said was the secret to their success.

"One night, we were playing the song, 'Land of a Thousand Dances,' when we saw a nice-looking woman doing a dance we had never seen before. While junior was still playing, he hollered down from the stage, 'What's that dance?' She said, 'It's the Shotgun!'"

The dance consisted of a finger, imitating a gun that shoots in various directions to the beat of a song. Dancers continued their already hip twisting, knee-poppin' moves with the addition of the "gun pointing." Thomas remembered members of the band laughing at the motion. It was then that Junior began replacing some of the words from the song they were playing with his own. "Shotgun. Shoot 'em fore he run now."

The song was a hit in the club and Helen encouraged them to approach Motown with it. They did. When Motown heard it, they added a crackling gunshot to the opening of the song and it topped the charts.

Berry Gordy mentioned Junior Walker in his book, *To Be Loved: The Music, The Magic, the Memories of Motown*. In the autobiography he wrote: "Junior was incredible. His saxophone sound was like nobody else's. The down-home feeling he and his band got when he sang and played his horn made it easy to produce him. All we had to do was get a good sound balance in the studio and just wait. He could put together some of the damnedest lyrics you'd ever heard and come out with a smash."

Some of those hilarious lyrics were in the hit, "Shotgun," written in 1965.

Shotgun/shoot 'em fo' he run now/Do the Jerk baby/Do the Jerk now./ Put on your high heel shoes/We're goin' down here now/And listen to 'em play the Blues/We're gonna do potatoes/We're gonna pick tomatoes.

With the enthusiasm of Berry, Junior told his band to, "pack your rags. We're going on the road."

They joined a Motown tour and performed for the first time at the Howard Theatre in Washington D.C. The tour circuit included cities such as New York, Philadelphia, and Chicago. During one-nighters, they traveled by bus or car. On longer performances (such as at the Apollo Theatre in Harlem) they performed up to three times a day.

"Shotgun," made the group a household name. It was a No. 1 single in 1965. They were now seen with the same admiration as other Motown artists on the tour such as *Martha Reeves and the Vandellas, The Velvelettes, The Contours, Smokey Robinson and the Miracles*, and Dionne Warwick.

That admiration came with a short leash when the group performed in the South. Thomas remembered being an 18-year-old Marine Corps soldier from the North when he got his first taste of segregation at a restaurant in Atlanta. Its sign read: "For whites only."

From left, Bill "Stix" Nicks, Willie Woods, and Fred Patton were the Rhythm Rockers who perform on the South Bend, Indiana dance show, Club 46, sponsored by WNDU. The group was the house band for the show from 1956-57. ~*Courtesy of Bill Nicks*~

Top and bottom: The Rhythm Rockers live on WNDU. Middle, Woods, James Graves, and Vic Thomas.

~Courtesy of Bill Nicks, Vic Thomas~

When the groups toured, they faced the racism when hotels allowed them to stay, but not use the pool. Some restaurants wouldn't serve them regardless of their hit records.

"Most of the concerts were 300-500 miles apart and we took the bus to get there," Thomas said. "Many southern segregated-style hotels didn't allow African Americans to check into their hotels, if they did, they had us come through the back door."

During one hotel episode in Nashville, the Yankee singers learned about the unspoken rule of the South when they went swimming in the hotel pool to relax.

"When we were on our way out, the hotel manager smiled a sly grin and said, 'stay out of the pool next time y'all out here.'" Thomas remembered the tone that made him shutter.

On the stage, however, the fans made them feel welcome, loved. They screamed and pulled at the group when they left venues. Thomas remembers one over-zealous fan who came after Junior. He often wore a necktie, but when one fan grabbed hold of it and he began to choke, he started to wear more clip-on ties.

Others who performed with Junior and the All Stars chuckled at the memories of them on stage. "I remember one show, where Junior fell off the stage at the Fox Theatre.

The El Grotto Lounge, 88 Kendall Street in Battle Creek, Michigan, was renovated and renamed, *Colors on the Corner*. It has since closed.

He fell off of the stage into the orchestra pit," said Martha Reeves of Martha Reeves and the Vandellas. "He got up, with his horn all bent, and kept playing, Shotgun!

"I hope one day somebody recognizes the magician he was—not *musician,* but magician. You couldn't follow Junior Walker. He would take a show whether he opened it or closed it. I loved me some Junior Walker," said Reeves, whose group's hits included hits such as "Heat Wave" and "Dancing in the Street."

Cal (Gill) Street of the Motown girls group, *The Velvelettes* also remembered Walker's enthusiasm and commitment. She remembered he has so much commitment to his fans that he was often fined by promoters for taking shows into overtime.

"He just couldn't stop," said Street whose group was founded after a talent show at Western Michigan University in Kalamazoo when she was in high school. "He would get to playing and that was it...time; who was coming on next, nothing mattered.

"When Junior went on stage all of us would laugh and say, we can go take a nap because it will be awhile before we get on–especially if he played "Shotgun" last. The crowd would want to hear it again and again."

While the crowd enjoyed the song, Thomas, the organist began to like it less.

"After a while of playing the song in concerts, hearing it on the radio, and then going to a bar and hearing it, I started to get kind of sick of hearing it," Thomas said.

Thomas also despised being fined for tardiness. One time

the 23-year-old didn't realize how serious the rules were until he received a letter stating he had two weeks to find other employment.

Sonny Holley, once with the Fayatons, would be called to take Thomas' place. He would now have another shot at Motown. Holley knew how to play the piano, but was given three days to learn how to use the Hammond B-3 organ.

Throughout the years, many musicians came and went from Junior's band. Bill Nicks, despite their issues as teenagers, maintained contact with his childhood friends and even substituted for the various drummers in the group throughout the years. Nicks played on the hit, "How Sweet It Is, To Be Loved By You," and throughout the years with other artists such as Sonny Stitt and Jackie Ivory.

Tony Washington left as the group's drummer and joined the Army just before "Shotgun" became a hit. After the military, he briefly sat in with the band but went on to serve with the Albion City and Pennfield Township Police Departments just outside of Battle Creek.

Bruce Richardson later joined the All Stars as its drummer. Richardson's family allowed Woods to live with them when Junior Walker first moved to Battle Creek from South Bend. Richardson was contracted into the group in 1963.

"I was young and excited about this," Richardson said. "I knew everything the band was playing. Junior offered me a job, but I didn't want to play with these old guys at first. Junior came by my house almost every day for about three weeks. Me and my mother finally gave in."

"When we went up to Detroit to sign the contract, I was too young to sign without a parent so my mother had to come," said Richardson who was 19 when he signed with Motown. "While we waited I was talking to one of the Supremes, trying to rap. Then (managers) called me in and said, 'You and your mother can come in and sign the contract now.' I was so embarrassed."

He later served in Vietnam not long after completing a recording with the All Stars. He was overseas when he heard their music and tried to convince his fellow soldiers that he was a member of that group.

"My mother would send my royalty checks to me. That proved it," Richardson said.

Anthony Payton and Arthur Langley also joined in the ever-changing band. Langley played before leaving to join Ike Turner's band for a short stint. James Graves replaced Richardson, and was the drummer for the band from around 1964-67. After his stint with the band, he performed with other local groups. Langley died in 1968 from injuries suffered during a car accident. He was just 27 years old and left behind a wife and son.

"Shotgun" put the group on the charts, but that song wouldn't be their last hit. Four other hits earned them gold records. Their singles "Hot Cha" and "What Does It Take to Win Your Love," was written by friend and former El Grotto headliner Johnny Bristol. Their albums "Soul Session" and "Road Runner," also showed great success. The group's style was unique. Even their clothing was classy as were the jumpsuits Woods had designed for the group to wear during one tour.

Victor Thomas shares an original tour program from
his days with the All Stars.~*Courtesy of Vic Thomas*~

GOVERNOR BILL CLINTON
Presidential Candidate

JUNIOR WALKER
Of the All Stars

You can see Governor Bill Clinton with the horn in his hands and he knows what he's doing with it. Take it from the Roadrunner, I know. . . I <u>can</u> blow a little bit.

Like the horn, we need to put America in Governor Bill Clinton's hands and maybe he can straighten this country out again!

I love America, don't you? Let's give Gov. Bill Clinton a chance! He may bring us new life and teach us to live together. Let's see if he can put America back on its feet again, where it belongs!

From one of the great Motown Legends . . . . .

Junior Walker and the All Stars

100

Junior Walker and the All Stars had many exciting moments together throughout their lifetime.
~Courtesy of Vic Thomas~

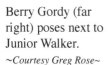

Berry Gordy (far right) poses next to Junior Walker.
~Courtesy Greg Rose~

The Velvelettes

The Velvelettes along with *Junior Walker and the All Stars*, represented Southwest Michigan at Motown. Standing from left, Mildred Gill, Bertha Barbee, Caldin "Cal" Gill; sitting from left, Betty Kelley, and Norma Barbee.~*Courtesy Cal Street*~

The Velvelettes began their musical careers in the next city west of Battle Creek, called Kalamazoo. They also had close ties to *Junior Walker and the All Stars* as they shared their talents on one another's recordings at Motown in Detroit.

The original group members included sisters Caldin "Cal" Gill and Mildred Gill, Cal's friend Betty Kelley (all of Kalamazoo), and cousins Bertha Barbee and Norma Barbee of Flint. Bertha met Mildred while playing piano in Davis Hall on the campus of Western Michigan University where the two were students.

In 1963 the two college friends formed a group with plans to enter an upcoming talent show sponsored by the Alpha Phi Alpha Fraternity. The show would be held at the Armory in downtown Kalamazoo, and winners would go home with the grand prize of $25. Cal and Betty (friends who were both in the ninth grade) were recruited to join Mildred, Bertha, and Norma.

They won, and after the show was approached by someone who would be the key to change their destinies. Robert Bullock had come from Detroit to attend the talent show. He told the girls that they had enough talent to audition for this uncle's company in Detroit. They laughed and were skeptical of this slick talker. He convinced them by showing him the labels of the records on the table of the disc jockey, pointing out such labels as Tamla, Gordy, and Tri-Phi, all part of Motown Records.

With excitement, the girls (Cal and Betty only in ninth grade) later pleaded with Mr. Gill to take them up to Detroit for an audition. He eventually caved in and agreed to take them on a Saturday. Mr. Gill and his son Charles, drove the girls on the two-lane highway to Detroit. Halfway there they were caught in a snowstorm. The normal two-hour drive took nearly six hours. One they finally arrived, they were told by a sassy receptionist that, "We don't have auditions on Saturdays."

The girls were crushed. Their father pleaded with the receptionist to give the girls a chance, especially since they had come all that way in a snowstorm from Kalamazoo.

"Kalama-who?" she replied, without sympathy for the girls who were on the verge of tears.

As they sat down in the front lobby, crying, a man walked through the door. Bertha looked up and recognized him. It was William "Mickey" Stevenson who had begun his own musical career while a student at Sherrod Middle School in Detroit years before.

Stevenson was the former member of a group called, *The Teen Toppers* who were a hit in a Detroit club, the Flame Club on John R. Road. Their hit, "Life of Ease," with the small Great Lakes Records, made them local celebrities. However, that was short lived as the company closed a short time later.

He went on to write and produce and had worked on a project with Bertha's former family group called, The Barbees while he was in Flint. That was the break they needed. Stevenson, now a writer and producer for Motown, gave the girls a shot. In 1963 they joined the company as the fourth girl group; following the Supremes, Martha Reeves and the Vandellas, and the Marvelettes.

Shortly after they signed, Betty was asked to join Martha

Reeves and the Vandellas. She remained a part of that group. In 1964 the Velvelettes released "Needle in a Haystack," which topped #19 on the National Billboard Magazine's Top 40. Their next hits, "He was Really Saying Something," These Things Will Keep Me Loving You," Lonely Lonely Girl Am I," and Bird in the Hand", also made Billboard's Top 100.

"Legendary Ladies of Motown"

Velvelettes throughout the years.~*Courtesy Cal Street*~

Al Green

Like the Velvelettes, other musicians in nearby towns became connected to Junior Walker and the El Grotto Lounge. While many local musicians made their mark in the music industry after honing their skills at the El Grotto, outside talent did as well. The (now, Reverend) Al Green was one of them.

Bobby Holley, left, Al Green ~*Courtesy of Bobby Holley*~

Green was born in 1946 in Dansby, Arkansas. His family later moved to Jacknash where his father worked as a sharecropper. The meager $800 a year his father grossed after adding up the $2.50 per day salary, lead him to pack his family up and head north to Grand Rapids, Michigan. Green's older brother had moved and worked for a refrigerator plant and boasted on the money that could be earned outside plantation crops.

The family's roots in the church led him to be a star soloist in the school choir, and later a member of a gospel group with his brothers. After expressing a desire to perform R&B music, Green was thrown out of the house. He quit school and eventually joined with friends in the group called *The Creations*.

One of the group's first gigs was in 1966 at the El Grotto Lounge, an approximately 45- minute drive from Grand Rapids.

Because Green was a mere 20 years old, he was not allowed into the club until performance time. He had to wait in the car where he could hear the house band setting the place "on fire" with their music. The talent of the house band's leader, Junior Walker left Green awestruck.

"I'd never seen anybody so cool, so sure of themselves and what they were doing, and I guess some of Junior Walker's attitude must have rubbed off on me, because I stepped up to the mic, all the nervous flutters in my stomach had disappeared. I knew who I was and I knew exactly what I was doing," Green said in his autobiography, *Take Me to The River.*

Green and his group performed other times at the club before they made recorded their hit, "Back up Train," which topped No. 41 on the charts. After years in the industry as a solo artist, Green became a hit with such songs as, "Tired of Being Alone," "Let's Stay Together," and "How Can You Mend a Broken Heart?"

By 1975 he had sold 35 million albums and had eight gold singles. But in 1977 after an incident with a woman led him to the hospital, he decided to become a minister and sing gospel. He purchased Full Gospel Tabernacle in Whitehaven, near Memphis. His gospel hits earned him two Grammy awards.

Green ventured onto the Motown label as did other El Grotto performers. While with Motown he recorded three number-one hits, which included, "Let's Stay Together" (1971), and "I'm Still in Love With You," and "You Ought To Be With Me" (1972).

Bobby Holley

As others were finding their fame and fortune through the stage at the El Grotto, Bobby Holley wanted that same glory. After watching his older brothers and sisters perform, he felt he was ready to strike his way into the industry.

In 1962 Holley got his first taste of the audience appreciation when he performed at the Battle Creek Central High School Band Follies. With the theatrics of James Brown (magnified five times) and the sultry singing style of Al Green, Holley felt nothing could stop him on his quest for his own gold record.

He auditioned for the *Ted Mack Amateur Hour* in New York. He won an opportunity to perform on the show, but could not afford the transportation costs to get there.

"See, back then, artists (unless they were with a record label) had to pay their own transportation, hotel, and food costs," said Holley. "It wasn't until you 'made it' that you would get those things paid for."

He graduated from high school and joined the military where he formed a band of fellow soldiers to perform on the Army base at Fort Rucker, Alabama, as well as in the area around the base. After the serving in the Army from 1966-68, he returned to school to study music theory and communications at Kellogg Community College, and later Western Michigan University.

Through it all, Holley still held on to his dream of being a star. He hoped his friends Jackey Beavers and Johnny Bristol, along with his brother, Sonny (who was an *All Star*), would be his key into Motown.

Clockwise: Bobby Holley
above at Battle Creek
Central. Holley's chart
position. Holley performs
with friends and as a solo
artist.

~Courtesy of Bobby Holley~

"I rode the bus to Motown one Saturday, and when I got there the woman at the front desk said, "We don't have auditions on Saturdays." Unlike the fate of the Velvelettes who had Motown producer, Mickey Stevenson to save their day, Holley had to take another path.

"When I came back home and everybody asked what happened (at the audition) I said, 'They liked me, and they want me to come back,'" Holley laughed. He did go back, however for a real audition.

"When I came back again, I was told I had one good song out of the three I performed. So I went back again, and again."

His determination did not persuade Motown producers to give him a chance, so he decided a new approach. He went back as part of a group, *The Willie Hollis Combo*. Holley said the group was signed, however, conflicts with their manager and Motown cost them their chance.

With the desire and no love from Motown, Holley tried a new label. He saw an advertisement in *Jet* magazine for artists to audition for Weis Records, he felt this could be his chance. Weis Records was located in Chicago and was a subsidiary of Stax Records.

The company, wanting new blood, signed Holley. In 1970 his songs, "Baby, I Love You," and "Movin' Dancer," climbed regional charts. It also made him a local hit.

"That little record was hot!" Holley said. "I was thinking of tours, photo shoots, sold out concerts. Boy, I was ready."

The potential of the song was one thing. The company's demise was yet another. In 1965, as the nation became divided on racial conflicts, Stax records worked to bring racial harmony into its studios. The company employed and recorded acts across color lines and launched the recording careers of those such as Isaac Hayes, Sam and Dave (hit "Hold On! I'm Comin'," "Soul Man"), and Otis Redding ("Dock of the Bay"). They also created subsidiary labels such as Volt, and Weis.

Unfortunately, the success did not last. Estelle Axton and Jim Stewart, who brought the company to its fame and glory, were bought and edged out. Stax went bankrupt in 1975.

Holley was devastated. Once again, he was without a record company while other artists on the label had the popularity to continue their careers with other record companies.

"I was the new kid on the block and my one record was not enough for anybody to pick me up," Holley said. "All I ever wanted to be was an entertainer."

Holley tried one more time to secure a record deal. In 1972 he signed to a small label, Bumpshop Records in Detroit. The relationship was short lived. He then took his future into his own hands and formed a band. The group would change names often as they searched for their identity. They were called *The Third Organization,* and *Earth Light.* He also would be featured with other such bands as the *Chapter Two, The Hollywood Swingers*, and *Main and the Sonic System.*

Through it all, as musicians sought to become rising stars– or were falling–they had a place at the El Grotto Lounge. It was a way to make a little extra money and continue experiencing a piece of the limelight. Holley's performances were memorable.

"I remember Bobby performing one night at the El Grotto," said Melvin Blackamore. "He was sliding on his back, jumping up and down; he made me tired just watching him. Next thing I know, he was wrapped up in toilet paper like a mummy. He ran out the back door and must have run down the street before he ran back through the front door, back on stage, and continued his song. Boy, it was something."

Holley began to use his electric personality for community activism in the city of Battle Creek. In 1992 he began efforts to have local heroes in the community honored. He established a plaque in honor of Donald Sherrod, the city's first black mayor. He raised money for a plaque in Montgomery's honor, which is located in Claude Evans Park in the Washington Heights neighborhood on the corner of Helen M. Montgomery and North Washington avenues.

In 1992 he was instrumental in renaming Roseneath Park at Howland and Roseneath avenues in honor of Julia Milner, longtime director of the Hamblin Community Center. He held a fund-raising campaign to place a plaque at Battle Creek Central Fieldhouse in honor of the late Bob James, a respected educator, coach and sports official who died in 1979.

With Holley's persistence, the late William E. Boards Jr., a commissioner and advocate for youth and education, was honored with a circular drive named after him at Leila Arboretum. He established scholarships in the names of respected community leaders and organized a rally to honor Al Leibert, a longtime coach and educator who did much to ease racial tension in the schools during the 1960s and 70s.

Holley's style of getting the community's attention has included attempts to tear down an abandoned home with an axe after a kindergartner was raped and murdered there. He has pulled a handmade coffin down the streets to protest the deaths of young African American men in the city; and has stood on a cross, in heat and cold, to protest drugs and violence in the city.

Holley's civic actions were criticized by some and applauded by others as the neighbors of South Wabash established a small park in his honor for his one-man attempt to demolish an abandoned home where a young girl was murdered.

Jimmy Lynch

Comedian Jimmy Lynch
with manager Vic LaVal Taylor ~*Courtesy of Tico Taylor*~

Through all the triumphs and trials of the 1960s and 70s, people needed relief–comic relief. The El Grotto Lounge provided that too. A combination of laughter and music was the key which led to the popularity of comedian Jimmie Lynch.

Comedian Jimmy Lynch recorded his live album, *Funky Tramp* on September 10, 1967, at the El Grotto Lounge for a sold out crowd. Known by many names such as Mr. Motion and The Tramp, Lynch mixed his love for music and comedy together. He took the stage complete with a baggy, ragged-appearing suit as a character much like a male version of the black female comedian of the time, Moms Mabley.

Not only did he perform, he came complete with his own band. In between a musical entrance and song, he performed what was considered an X-rated dialog of jokes and stories.

Lynch was born in 1937 in Acmar, Alabama. The Alabama-born entertainer began his career as a singer. His high school group, "The Kings," performed on television and at nightclubs. At one night club, he was given a chance to perform; the manager needed someone to make the people laugh. Lynch created a tramp-like costume (mainly to hide his youthful appearance) and begin to "clown."

In 1957 he moved to Fort Wayne, Indiana where he performed with a gospel group, the *Angelic Harmonizers*. But, his love for the nightclub scene overwhelmed his spiritual attempts, and he returned to the clubs in 1967; redefining his Tramp character.

"Jimmy paved the way for others to be themselves at a time when people needed somebody to laugh at," said Tico Taylor, whose father was Lynch's promoter and manager.

Taylor's father, Vic "LaVal" Taylor, was known for promoting shows with big name stars in his hometown of Kalamazoo and the nation. LaVal's brother lived in San Francisco, California, where he owned a record company. He needed someone to distribute his records in the Midwest and east coast and LaVal would be the one for the job. LaVal had ten children to feed and this, along with his odd jobs as chauffeur and postal worker, was a welcome addition to his finances.

He promoted shows such as Ike and Tina Turner and Chick Willis, whose song, "Stoop Down Baby, Let Your Daddy See," would be distributed by the LaVal Record label. Lynch was his biggest moneymaker as he sold more than one million albums (according to Tico). LaVal was responsible for getting the records to jukeboxes across the region. The first album his father sold was at a barbershop in Battle Creek.

"My father and Jimmy didn't always see eye to eye on his career," Tico said. "Jimmie wanted to be a singer, but he was better at telling jokes. He would break up his routine after a joke with a song and dance. People just wanted to hear jokes when he came out and his singing broke the momentum as far as my father was concerned."

In 1968 the *Funky Tramp* album was top seller according to Coleman's Records in California. On September 23 of that year, it was No. 1; beating out, *At the Apollo* by James Brown and *Aretha Now* by Aretha Franklin. Since Lynch was a hit in California, he decided to take on the Sunshine State. Soon after his arrival, he met a man who would take him to the big screen.

He became friends with comedian Rudy Ray Moore who was best known for his blaxploitation films of the 1970s. Moore's film's often starred himself as the character, Dolemite. The two comedians shared the same raunchy style, which made them the perfect match.

Moore saw Lynch as one of the early comedians who performed 'four-letter comedy,' similar to the styles of Redd Roxx and later, Richard Pryor. Lynch played in Moore's latest movie, "The Return of Dolemite," in 2001. Prior to that, he had released five comedy albums of his own.

Eventually, Lynch left acting to work as tour manager and emcee for many famous blues artists like Bobby "Blue" Bland, ZZ Hill, Tyrone Davis, Millie Jackson, Patti LaBelle and Johnny Taylor.

Bottom, Jimmy Lynch's tour wagon.
Top from left movie posters featuring movies
Lynch performed in during the 1970's. Middle left,
Lynch in "Petey Wheatstraw" and an early comedy album.
~*Courtesy of Tico Taylor*~

The Three Sounds

Bill Dowdy, center,
poses with Gene Harris
and Andy Simpkins
as Blue Note reording
artists, *The Three
Sounds*.
~Courtesy of Bill Dowdy~

While hip shakin' and grinding hits were hits among many who frequented the El Grotto Lounge, musicians who wanted to perfect their craft in the areas of jazz, would also be made to feel at home on its stage.

One of those musicians was Bobby Parker, an accomplished bass player. He expressed the idea that jazz could work at the lounge and organized a jazz night. The native of Albion, Michigan, Parker had learned how to play the bass from his parents who were musicians. Throughout his life, he performed with various groups and eventually formed his own, *The Bobby Parker Trio*.

After realizing the one night a week the El Grotto or Bellman's and Waiter's Club dedicated to jazz wasn't enough, he opened his own jazz club in the early 1970s called *Bobby's Place*. The club, perched on a small lot on Main Street, allowed jazz lovers to congregate and participate in a jam session with area musicians.

One of those frequent performers was Bill Dowdy. He made Battle Creek his home after a stint with the classy Blue Note Records trio, *The Three Sounds*. Born in 1933 in Osceola, Arkansas, Dowdy and his family moved to Benton Harbor, Michigan where they were encouraged to learn to play instruments. His younger brother bought a $40 piano with money he saved from restaurant work, and Dowdy was determined to learn how to play.

While in high school, he and his friends formed a group called, *The Club 49 Trio*. Although Dowdy wanted to play piano for the group, his friend, Gene Harris was the more skilled with the 88-key instrument. Dowdy was persuaded to use his skills as the band's drummer. The trio entered the high school band follies and was so well received that they were given a 30-minute spot to perform every Saturday on local radio station, WHFB. They used their radio experience to compete at the famous Morris B. Saks radio and TV talent show. And while they came close to winning, they left empty-handed.

After graduating from high school in the 1950s, Dowdy went on to play with the Rupert Harris Band. He later served in the Army Tank Corps where he sat in on jam sessions with fellow soldiers. There he met Cannonball Adderly. After his discharge from the Army in 1954, Dowdy studied music at Roosevelt University in Chicago and Knapp's School of Percussion.

While in the Windy City, he performed session work at a music studio with Eddie Boyd, Willie Mabon, the Moonglows, and the Flamingos. He played at the city's Beehive Jazz Club with such jazz greats as Johnny Griffin, J.J. Johnson, Sonny Stitt, Gene Ammons, and Joe Williams. In addition, he perfected his craft with drum lessons with Oliver Coleman, one of the most popular drum teachers on Chicago's Southside.

Dowdy was just 22 years old when he landed a job as house drummer for Chicago's Cotton Club where he played with Junior Mance, Wilbert Ware, Eddie Harris, John Jenkins, John Gilmore, and Clifford Jordan.

In 1956 Harris called Dowdy from South Bend to invite him to participate in a band with saxophonist Lonnie "The Sound" Walker, and Andy Simpkins on bass. They performed at the Club Chez Paris under the name, *The Four Sounds*.

Simpkins, born in Richmond, Indiana in 1932, was originally a clarinetist and pianist. Between his years at Wilburforce College and his Army stint that he discovered the bass and loved it. When Walker decided to leave the group they became leaving *The Three Sounds.*

In 1958 while playing in a Washington D.C. jazz club, they caught the attention of Mercer Ellington, the son of Duke Ellington. Mercer had brought in the owners of the jazz recording label, Blue Note, to hear the trio. Alfred Lyons and Francis Wolf signed the group immediately.

The newbies to the label also served as the rhythm section for a Nat Adderly quintet date on Riverside with Johnny Griffin. They recorded a third session of their own and an album with Lou Donaldson entitled *LD Plus Three*.

From September 1959 through June 1962 trio went to Rudy Van Gelder's on 14 different occasions under the auspices of Blue Note Records, to record a vast amount of material. On March 8, 1962, they recorded a number of tunes, which appeared on such albums as *Black Orchid,* and *Out Of This World*.

The trio left Blue Note Records in mid-1962 and recorded a number of albums for Mercury and Verve before returning to Blue Note in October of 1966. While with Blue Note they performed backup for such artists as Nancy Wilson, Ernestine Anderson, Al Hibbler, Ben Webster and Coleman Hawkins.

Over the next ten-years, *The Three Sounds* recorded more than 24 albums-all considered classics. Their best-known Blue Note recordings are "Black Orchid," "Feelin' Good," "Moods," "Three Moods," "Blue Hour" with Stanley Turrentine, "The Three Sounds" with Lou Donaldson, and "The Best of the Three Sounds." They also recorded "Branching Out with Nat Adderly and Johnny Griffin," for Riverside, "Anita O'Day and The Three Sounds," for Verve, and "Beautiful Friendship," for Limelight.

Dowdy and his friends opened for such artists as Miles

Davis, John Coltrane, Aretha Franklin, Ahmad Jamal, and Shirley Horn. They graced the stages of Bird Land, Apollo Theatre, the Village Vanguard, and the Village Gate in New York City, Pep's Show Bar in Philadelphia, Don King's in Cleveland, the Lighthouse in Los Angeles, the Jazz Workshop in San Francisco, and Jazz Showcase in Chicago.

Through all of the success personal issues tainted their relationships and Dowdy left in early 1967. He was replaced by longtime Jimmy Smith drummer Donald Bailey. By the end of 1968, both Simpkins and Bailey were gone. After replacing various members, the name "The Three Sounds" also dissipated in the early 1970s. Gene Harris, the group's pianist and leader, continued to record for Blue Note until 1976. He added an array of electronic keyboards to his sound, and in the early 1980s he collaborated on albums with a variety of artists and led a trio with bassist Ray Brown.

After leaving the group, Dowdy returned to Battle Creek where he had family. His career slowed considerably and he took on a job as manager of Grinnell's Music Store, and Farrow's Music. In 1969 he opened Bill Dowdy Music Enterprises, which sold instruments, sheet and recorded music and offered music lessons. He owned and operated the business until 1983. Various students ventured into Dowdy's studio such as Anthony Payton, later played with *Junior Walker and the All Stars*.

Dowdy became active in the community and served as president of the Downtown Development Association and the Calhoun County Black Business and Professional Association. He served on the boards of directors for the Battle Creek Area Chamber of Commerce, Battle Creek Symphony, and as a charter member of Battle Creek Unlimited business development company.

Club '49 Trio

With a theme of "Slow Blues," three Benton Harbor high school Negro youths, the "Club '49 Trio," will take to the air with a program of their own, starting Saturday, March 12, to be ___ ___ urday afternoon ___. ___he trio, which ___ this winter for ___ber high school ___ William Dow___ er, and dru a___ones, 17, bass: ___ire, 15, at the

Haire has been playing boogie since his fifth grade days, when his teacher discovered him at the school piano, picking out "Way Down South" by ear as a child prodigy he made a number of appearances in public in Benton Harbor and vicinity.

The trio expects to feature original numbers of its own, which include "Bass Boogie," "Prom Boogie," and the "Gene Haire Blues." Known as Bill, Gene and Jane, the three play regularly together each weekend at a local restaurant.

The Three Sounds Gene Harris, Bill Dowdy, and Andy Simpkins, began their musical careers in high school in Benton Harbor, Michigan. eventually travel the world as Blue Note Recording artists.

~Courtesy of Janie Harris~

Bottom right, Abby Lincoln, a former Kalamazoo resident, once performed with the group.

~Painting by James Palmore~

125

He used his talents to give private lessons and conducted master classes at Western Michigan University, Kellogg Community College, and Michigan State University. He organized *Bill Dowdy's Trio Plus*, which performed for various community and private events. Although Dowdy could earn a living teaching music lessons, he gave free lessons to local neighborhood kids.

"The kids would come over and ask me if I could teach them how to play the drums," Dowdy said. "We would meet in my garage and we would get big white buckets and some drum sticks and they would have fun."

Word of Dowdy's free lessons spread to a local housing complex. Its program coordinator planned to write a grant for drums and supplies if Dowdy agreed to give the students free lessons. He agreed. In 1994, with the support of non-profit Substance Abuse Council, Dowdy's *Drumming for Life* was born. They received funds and extra support through the agency, which concentrated on youth drug-prevention programs. Dowdy continued to use his expertise as an instructor for the Battle Creek Music School.

End of an Era

African Americans in Battle Creek reached the 1970s with new hopes and dreams. They had dreams of well-paying careers, adequate housing, and an equal opportunity for education. In the 70s and 80s, even the Bellman's and Waiter's Club began to lose steam and some of its older members.

They attempted to bring in younger guests with Ladies Nights and dance contests. In the early 1980s the city began plans to demolish the club and other buildings in the area for a parking structure. By 1985 the club had less than 200 members.

Despite reports that the city would relocate the club, it did not. And in 1995 the Bellman's and Waiter's Club was demolished. The building, once a Salvation Army and Armed Services office before becoming a club, was 100 years old.

Just as the economic and social climate began to take a turn for the better, violence began to plague the El Grotto Lounge. For years, the club would find a frequent spot in the newspapers for a shooting, stabbing, fight or other altercation, which occurred at the address. "A younger crowd was coming on the scene and they were looking for something other than just having a good time," said Melvin Evans, the club's bartender and brother of owner, Helen.

In 1972 Robert "Snap" Montgomery died after a short illness. He and Helen had operated the club together for more than twenty years. She was now left to run the club with the help of her brother, Melvin. Together they attempted to appease their new, younger audience. They offered a local version of the television show, "The Gong Show." They held "Big Legs" and "Hot Pants" contests, but nothing seemed to work for their patrons.

Helen attempted to keep that personal touch that made the club popular. She talked to customers and knew many of them by name. Her ties with former performers stayed strong as well. According to Melvin, after Al Green became a popular artist worldwide, he visited the club on his way through town and gave Helen a letter of thanks for giving him his start at the club.

All who knew Mrs. Helen proclaim she treated those who worked for the club and its customers like family. She often showed her love by cooking for them. In 1989, while she prepared to barbecue for her staff, an unexpected flare of the fire caught hold of her clothing. She died a week later from the severity of the burns.

Helen would be missed by thousands in the community who knew her from decades of attending her club, or working with her on the Battle Creek Community Relations Committee, the People's Action Committee, the local NAACP, the Southwestern Michigan Urban League, the Calhoun County Business Professional Association, Ada Chapter of the Order of the Eastern Star, or Mt. Zion A.M.E. Church.

After her death, her family attempted to keep the club going but lost it due to back taxes. In 1993 the club was sold for $1 to a local couple who put in more than $60,000 to renovate the club. They renamed it *Colors on the Corner* as it was rightly named for its pastel exterior design. That couple also lost the club due to financial difficulties, and it 2003 it was again for sale.

While money may have led to the demise of the club, many say it was the personality of Snap and Helen that was the secret to its success. The El Grotto was the foundation many artists needed. Many of those who performed on the tiny stage, continued to perform with those who they have known for decades.

Drummer Duane Griffin played at area clubs from 1954 to 1980 before he left the music world to run the family's contract cleaning business, Superb Cleaning. He played drums with house bands, which backed up visiting artists such as B.B. King and Mary Wells.

Samuel "Singing Sam" Moore, made frequent appearances at clubs throughout the city. He was born in Perry County, Alabama. His family moved to Chicago and later Battle Creek where he became friends with many others who wanted to become performers. Moore went on to perform with vocalist Ronnie Laws, and has been an opening act for those like B.B. King and Bobby Rush. He also teamed with friend and fellow Blues musician Lou Wilson, to play guitar and coproduce with Wilson's *Today's People*.

Wilson, who once organized several Do-Wop groups in Battle Creek (seeing some of his group members become famous) was born in Senatobia, Mississippi. He came to Battle Creek in 1951. In 1953 he enlisted in the military where he served until 1955.

When he returned, he used his flair for music and organizing groups to form a group of students called *The Vandalist*. He would continue for decades as a member of *The Shifters*, *Jessie Blackford and the Diamond Aces*, and *Wade Flemons and the Newcomer* where friendship deteriorated when Flemons went on to success without Wilson or the others.

In 1965 he started *The Esquires,* which consisted of Sam Moore, Walter Garrett and LeShurn Houston. They recorded a song, "Shotgun in a Slain" for Magic City recording company. It was never released. Alfred Birch and Earl English later joined the band. Wilson, determined to find the right group, formed *Lou Wilson and Charlotte Wanzer.*

They recorded "This Love is Getting Deeper," and "We Need to Get Together," on the Kent Label in California. The group moved to Columbia Records where they recorded, "Talking About Poor Folks Talking About My Folks," and "Got to Be Me." Wanzer moved on to a solo career, and the group changed to *Lou Wilson and Today's People.*

Members from former groups and new additions were added to include, Alice Wilson, LeShurn Houston, Walter Garrett, Byron Jackman, and Warren Johnson. Under their Crew Records label, they released three CDs, which included, *On the Right Track, True Blues,* and *Prime Time Blues.*

The company has since merged with a larger company, Momentum Recording Company. Their CD, *True Blues,* was #4 on the WNWN 1560 AM (Kalamazoo, Michigan) most requested songs of the month in November of 1998.

What Became of a Dream?

Wilson was one of the few who started at the Hamblin Community Center and persevered to take a passion for performing to a higher level. These musicians carried the dreams for a new opportunity just as the fugitive slaves and freedmen who came to the city in its inception sought a better way of life.

In both cases, some had their dreams dashed before they even began. Others took what they learned from those who came before them, taking the good and bad, to make what they could of their own dreams.

What was the formula of success for those who did achieve their dreams? Was it Julia Milner and her leadership at the Hamblin Community Center? The center that seemed to be a bridge for both black and white children to come together in athletic competition closed for what seemed to be a solution to segregation.

In 1962 the Civil Rights movement led many organizations toward integration. The Battle Creek NAACP along with the Battle Creek Human Relations Commission, and Area Council on Human Relations, made a motion to the city to discontinue all youth activities held at various sites

Lou Wilson's musical genius helped cultivate many Battle Creek artists who held successful careers in the music industry. Wilson has been honored and recognized in Battle Creek for his role as a musical leader.

~Photo provided by Lou Wilson. ~

Top: Eddie Hollis, who contributed his song-writing talents to those such as Junior Walker and Bobby Holley. Above: Duane Griffin backed many artists who visited the area such as B.B.King and Mary Wells.
~*Photos by Sean Hollins.* ~

throughout the community. Their goal was to integrate the youth in other programs throughout the city.

"I don't know why they did that," Ernie Townsend said. "The Hamblin Community Center was a place for all children to come together. It wasn't just for blacks only. Closing the center was the biggest mistake for the community. After that, there really was no place else like it, ever, for young people to go."

The center continued to go through transformations. In 1964 it became the Senior Citizen Center. In 1974 the senior center was relocated into the Valentine Center, named for the city's first black vice mayor, Clark Valentine.

Over the years the building was used by various businesses and was even a roller skating rink for small children. It still stands at 242 Hamblin Avenue.

Not many are alive today who knew the Hamblin Community Center when it held dances that had boys and girls dancing to swing. Not many know of Battle Creek native, Melvin "Sy" Oliver, who was still active in the 1970s and 1980s as the leader of his own band at the Rainbow Room in New York City. In 1974, he created a month-long tribute to Big Band leader Jimmie Lunceford and the music which bridged the racial divide.

Oliver retired as a band leader in 1984. He briefly joined an overseas traveling band where he played trumpet; something he had not done since leaving Lunceford's band in 1939. His life in music had been unplanned, yet highly successful, and lead to hundreds of popular compositions for dozens of musicians. He was recognized by Jazz organizations for his contribution to the music industry. On May 28, 1988, Oliver died of lung cancer in Mount Sinai Hospital in New York.

Having learned music and composition, without formal teaching, Oliver goes down in music history as one of the top arrangers and composers of his time.

Not many who pass by the beautifully redesigned Battle Creek Central High School know the history of one of its students who had his shot at fame–Wade Flemons. After Wade Flemons broke from *Earth, Wind, and Fire* to form his own group, *Colors*, he never saw another hit of any kind.

Maurice White however, took *Earth, Wind, and Fire* on to become a group of younger, moldable artists in 1972. They made hit after hit, and soon had a Top 40 R&B hit with their song, "Evil."

The next year the group hit big with, "Mighty Mighty," and the following year their tune, "That's the Way of the World," reached No. 1 on the Billboards Singles chart, earning them their first of many Grammy awards.

Flemons watched the group's success from the sidelines.

"Wade was always on the verge of something big, and then, something would go wrong," said longtime friend Jerry Butler. "There is a difference between *show* and *business*, and Wade was one who didn't always realize the *business* was just as important as the *show*."

He remained in California for several years where he worked as a bus driver. He returned to Battle Creek in the early 1990s and toured with other local musicians under the fame of his hit, "Here I Stand."

In 1993 he talked with his son Brian, about recording again. He wanted to team with his son with the hope of returning to the industry. Two days after that conversation with his son, Flemons died of a heart attack. He was just 53 years old.

Earth, Wind and Fire continued their rise to the top, earning more than six consecutive multi-platinum albums and eight gold singles. Their style, a mix of funk, gospel, Latin, Jazz and African styles, coupled with their flamboyant, outrageous stage dynamics, led them to perform for years in sold out concerts. In 2000, they were inducted into the *Rock and Roll Hall of Fame*.

White did not attend Flemons' funeral in Battle Creek, and heard about the death through a fan.

"I felt kind of bad because we didn't get a chance to straighten stuff out," he said.

Not many who go through the Washington Heights area down Kendall even know the history of the El Grotto Lounge. They don't know of Junior Walker and the All Stars and the many musicians who got their chance with the band.

While band members continued to change, Junior remained the lead of *Junior Walker and the All Stars*. For decades he recorded other albums and toured the world with his saxophone. In 1981, he joined rock band, *Foreigner,* on their song, "Urgent," where Junior blew a sax solo that propelled him back into the spotlight.

In 1988 Junior made a movie debut in *Tapeheads,* which starred John Cusack and Tim Robbins. The movie featured the stars as they attempted to create a music video company. Junior, along with Sam Moore (formerly of Stax Records duo Sam and Dave), played has-been musicians who the men wanted to re-launch into public with a fresh video exemplifying their blues style.

Junior also had several guest appearances on *The David Letterman Show* during this time in promotion of the movie. In 1989 he helped young governor Bill Clinton, in his run for president. Junior and Clinton (both Arkansas natives), played the saxophone together during a campaign event. A photo of the jam session was used on a campaign flyer. The photo of the two signed by Clinton reads: "To Jr. Walker–a great son of Arkansas who made my year!"

Junior continued to perform until he suffered health issues. He had a kidney removed and in 1993 and later was diagnosed with cancer. He settled down in Battle Creek with his family. Friends, Thomas, Woods, and brothers Sonny and Bobby Holley were by his bedside the night before his death in November 1995.

The group's signature song, "Shotgun," remains a hit, and has been used in various movies and television shows such as in the theme of *Saturday Night Live, The Cosby Show*, and Spike Lee's movie, *Malcolm X*.

In 1985, "Shotgun" earned the group a gold record for it sales of more than 500,000 copies. That year, Woods, quoted in an article in the *Battle Creek Enquirer* (1985), encouraged the community to support local musicians just as they had been supported by the owners of the El Grotto Lounge.

Woods continued to perform with other local bands such as *Bobby Holley's Earthlight Band*, and never forgot the kindness of the Helen and Snap Montgomery for their financial and parental-like support.

"It's discouraging to those who have the ability but not the support of fellow musicians," Woods said. "We have a lot of great musicians here. All they need is the extra push that it takes–no matter how hard it is."

Woods organized his own local groups named, *The Apaches* and *Equinox*. He wanted to tour again and began to write songs. He won fourth place in a national song writing contest for his song, "Karen", named for his wife. Unfortunately, time was not on his side. He died in 1997 before making that dream come true.

Karen, remembers Woods for his perseverance and gentle spirit with everyone he met. They had met in 1980; both had been divorced and had eight children between them. "Willie practiced daily. He never held a 9-to-5 job. Performing was his life," Karen said. "There was always so much more he wanted to do musically; so much he wanted to learn. He was definitely an artist. His whole life was structured around music. It didn't matter what time of the day or night it was, if he had an idea for a song he would get up and write it down."

As riders boarded the city bus in Battle Creek driven by Victor Thomas, they may not have known he still received royalties from Motown Records for this role in Junior Walker's band as an organ player.

Thomas retired from the City of Battle Creek as a city bus driver. He never joined another band or performed after being released the group. He was bitter regarding the whole experience and turned his focused toward religion; leaving secular music in his past. He opened his archives to share his memories for this book. Later, he suffered from dementia before his death in 2010.

Sonny Holley, who followed Thomas in the band, continue to gain success and see the world as an All Star. He was later nominated by his brother Bobby for a Key to the City of Battle Creek for his role in music history. After receiving the award, a community celebration was held to recognize Sonny for his talent, and contribution to the world of music.

Those who pass by Fort Custer military base in Battle Creek may not even remember the days when it was a bustling base of soldiers and family housing. They may not even know of the soldiers Jackey Beavers and Johnny Bristol, who served duo roles in the city–soldiers by day, and entertainers at the El Grotto Lounge by night.

Their careers were perhaps the most successful of all those who called Battle Creek their home. The duo's song writing proved fruitful with their hit for Diana Ross and the Supremes, so, they gave their partnership another try.

This time, they wrote the hit, "Do You See My Love Growing," for their friend and fellow Motown artist, Junior Walker. But, times were changing.

It had become the turbulent 60s and 70s, and the country was at odds regarding integration, Vietnam, and the lack of employment and political advancement opportunities. Lunch counter sit-ins, the Montgomery Bus Boycott, the assassination of the Rev. Martin Luther King Jr. and dozens of race riots across the country were causing a friction between the races, which would define the times as the Civil Rights Era.

Although Beavers led an integrated band, one booking to perform at a festival in Michigan brought light to the reality of things going on around the country. Once he and his band arrived, they were not allowed to play.

"For entertainers, it was sometimes overlooked that you were black," Beavers said. "But during the Civil Rights Movement, people started to notice I was Black *first*, entertainer *second*."

Beavers became disheartened by these types of experiences and the constant road trips. He and his wife decided to move back to his hometown, Cartersville, Georgia.

In the meantime, Bristol remained with the Motown family. He brought on other artists and wrote and produced with Harvey Fuqua. Together they created hits for such Motown artists as Stevie Wonder, *The Velvelettes*, Michael Jackson, Marvin Gaye, and Smokey Robinson.

In 1974 Bristol left Motown to become a solo artist for MGM Records. His single, "Hang On In There Baby," went to No. 2 on the R&B charts, and No. 8 on the pop charts. He earned a gold album, a gold single, and two Grammy nominations for works created in 1974-75. In 1976, "Do it to my Mind," hit No. 5 on the charts.

For Beavers, the South led to other ventures in music. He opened a nightclub with his brother and named it, Brothers 3. His band, *The Continental Showstoppers* performed between other acts. However, in 1974 the energy crises created a gasoline shortage and prices went from 17 cents to $1 a gallon. Beavers felt it was because of this, and other economic hardships in the nation, that people drove less for recreation. His club's attendance suffered because of it.

Although still performing and working the club with his brother, Beavers felt something in his life was missing. He received what he believed a sign from God to leave the club scene altogether. His truck, used to transport the band to gigs broke down. A booking agent gave him a bogus check after a performance. And the atmosphere in his own club became dissatisfying.

"One night the gambling in the dressing room, bump and grind dancing, and cursing was just too much. I just wanted to get out of there and never perform for the devil again," Beaver said.

He had roots in the church, and his father still was a preacher. In 1975 Beavers decided to enter the ministry. In 1983, while serving as pastor at Baptist Church in Cartersville, he became executive assistant to the state's Governor Joe Frank Harris. He held that position until 1991.

Beavers later became Bishop Beavers, and lead his own church. He continued to perform, for the Lord, and created the song, "Devil's Stomp." The song made its debut at No. 35 on the Cash Box Gospel charts in August of 1991. The video performance of the song also was a top video on the *Bobby Jones Top 5* video show featured on Black Entertainment Television (BET).

Johnny Bristol died in 2004 before completing a gospel album of his own. Beavers died in 2008.

New Generation

While those who set the tempo for young musicians have died, and in some cases have never received recognition for their work, younger musicians continue to keep the follow their dreams of musical success.

Battle Creek's Bruce Broadus, and friend Debra Jen Hurd called themselves, "Damian Dame." Broadus was born in Marshall, Michigan to parents Bruce and Zona. Not long after moving to Battle Creek, 4-year-old Bruce was given a drum set by his godparents.

His constant banging led to his mother setting it up in the garage. He was later introduced to the piano when his uncle, Dwayne Grant (who once played for Gospel artist Andre Crouch), gave him a piano when he was 8 years old.

"He took lessons, and didn't want to listen to the teacher," said his mother, Zona. "He had a gift of playing instruments... and on his own, he mastered the song, "Ben," by the Jackson 5.

He was known for disappearing at school and being found in the music room. After high school, he formed a singing group called, Shyboy, and they moved to Kalamazoo. He soon ventured to California where he met Debra Jen Hurd. They called themselves, Damian Dame.

He wrote the music, and they presented a demo tape to producers L.A. Reid and Babyface Edwards. The duo was immediately signed as the first acts on the LaFace label.

As the first group on the label, the two received all of the producers' attention. In July 1994 their first single, "Exclusivity," was #10 on the charts.

"I never thought anything would come of his music," said Zona, who holds a prized gold record her son earned. She was often at his performances when he came to the state, and watched him on *Soul Train, Showtime at the Apollo*, and other programs.

The duet had others hits such as, "Right Down to It," and "Gotta Learn My Rhythm." However, their careers were short lived. His partner was killed in a car accident on June 27, 1994. She was 35 years old. With his partner gone, the company concentrated on other artists, however, he did record the song, "Reversal of a Dog," featured on the Boomerang soundtrack.

In 1995 he moved to Mama Janie Music (ASCAP) Chip Records where he recorded the LP Damian *199sex*. A week after it was released, he died of colon cancer three years to the date of his former partner, Hurd.

While many of the Battle Creek artist aimed for record labels, Eric Riley, a 1973 graduate of Battle Creek Central High School, headed toward Broadway.

Riley was a hit during the popular Follies at Central. He met a teacher who became a mentor and encourager of the arts. She led him and friends to audition for the play, "Hair," at the Barn Theatre in Augusta, a few miles from Battle Creek.

They did, and it sparked an interest in Riley that would catch on fire. As an honor student, Riley received a full scholarship to the University of Michigan. He could study law, engineering or pre-med. He selected law.

"I chose this one because it was the closest to allowing me to take some acting or theatre classes as electives," he said.

In the meantime, he participated in plays at the Barn Theatre for the next two years. He performed in such plays as Godspell, and Jesus Christ Superstar, under his belt when he earned what he had been waiting on. After so many hours in the theatre, performers could earn equity cards, to license them to perform anywhere.

"Once I had that, it was over for school. I told my mother that I was leaving for New York. She didn't believe me, nobody did. But, I had been working with actors at the Barn Theatre who were from New York. I had my ride and everything, and left in 1975 after two years of college. I've never looked back."

His success began immediately in the New York Harlem Dance Theater where he worked for three months. He immediately joined an overseas production of *Hair*, in Spain from 1975-76. The rest is a whirlwind.

From 1976 to 1995, he performed on and off Broadway with Yul Brynner in *The King and I, The All Night Strut,* in Ford's Theater in Washington D.C., *A Chorus Line, Ain't Misbehavin', Dreamgirls, Once on This Island* (Broadway), *Weird Romance*, (Off Broadway), *A Christmas Carol* at Madison Square Garden, *Anyone Can Whistle,* at Carnegie Hall, 2001 Langston Hughes' *Little Ham* (Director Off Broadway).

His years in the theater came to a halt after his mother died in 2001, and his father less than two years later.

"It was then I had to decide, what was really important to me at this stage in my life. I was 50, and as far as theater, I had 'been there, done that.'"

Riley decided to go back to school. He earned a Bachelors of Arts degree in New York from The New School, and (at the time of original publication in 2003) was completing a master's degree in International Affairs.

Bruce Broadus & Debra Hurd.
~Courtesy of Zona Broadus~

Eric Riley actor/dancer/singer
~Photo provided by Eric Riley~

Afterword

Small towns and large cities throughout the country have stories of successful citizens who were determined to follow their dreams at all costs. Those stories are what keep communities alive and thriving.

Battle Creek is no different. Its people worked toward economic and political freedoms. Helen and Snap Montgomery were two of them. While I never had a chance to meet them, I feel their loving spirit in all those who talk about her. I feel for the children of today who do not have someone like "Miss Helen," to look up to for support as an entertainer.

Helen's brother, Melvin (who along with Bobby Holley was instrumental in this book project) summed up the club and its role in the community by saying:

"I remember something a Fort Custer soldier said on his last night at the club before being transferred to another base and I will never forget it. He said, 'Things may come. And things may go. But I'll never forget the El Grotto.'"

I too will never forget the El Grotto; not the building itself, but those who graced its stages. My musical journey with one city began in 1993. It was then, as a young reporter in Battle Creek, Michigan, that famous musicians from the Do Wop era embarked upon the city to attend a funeral of a man named Wade Flemons. I learn that Flemons was a musical icon in the city, and had recorded the song, "Here I Stand", a popular hit in 1958. I was schooled on the others who made musical fame in the city, and those whose musical fame was somehow connected to Battle Creek; those like *Junior Walker and the All Stars*, Al Green, Bill Dowdy of Blue Note Records, and Big Band composer Sy Oliver, all many others.

During a ten-year research journey, I narrowly missed opportunities to interview key artists such as Junior Walker and his guitar player, Willie Woods. I would, however, meet a fantastic group of musicians, historians, club owners, and music fans from the city who would assist me in completing the book, *Here I Stand* in 2003.

Those in the city embraced the story of the musicians whose stories had been left silent in the scrapbooks they tucked away in their attics and basements. No one had shown an interest in their lives touring the world or the stories of friendships lost and found because of their love for their craft.

Heritage Battle Creek, a nonprofit historical society in the city, partnered with me to hold several panel discussions with the musicians at the colleges and elementary schools. We organized a free concert for the community at W. K. Kellogg Auditorium, that would feature the musicians on stage together for the first time in decades.

It was a bittersweet moment; the performers, the audience dancing in their seats to songs that reminded them of simpler times. After the release of the book in 2003, Bobby Holley said something that made the entire project worth it. He said, "Now, because of this book, no one will forget us."

That made all the long nights of writing worth it. It made

the long hours of making sure I listened to as many of the musicians as I could worth it. It made all the time we spent talking about times I wish I could have lived in, worth it.

Since 2003 some of the musicians who I spoke with for this project have passed away. Jackey and Johnny have passed on, so has Earnie Townsend, Melvin Blackmore, and others who provided pieces of the history puzzle that help bring this story together.

Many entertainers who graced the stage at the El Grotto did not earn fame and fortune. Those who did (or didn't) credit the support of the Montgomery duo for giving them a chance.

I also have tried to keep the legacy of Helen Montgomery alive through the Helen Montgomery Musicians Fund housed at the Battle Creek Community Foundation. This fund is for young musicians who need anything from music lessons to plane fare for an audition...things Robert and Helen Montgomery would have reached into their pockets to give.

Inset: In 2001 Jim Cummings, far right, opened his home and studio for an initial interview with musicians. They include from left: Sonny Holley, Bobby Holley, Bill "Sticks" Nicks, (back), Melvin Evans, Melvin Blackamore, Lou Wilson, Will Ready, and Bill Dowdy. Photo by Sean Hollins (2001).

Narrative Bibliography

In writing this book I learned that many of the subjects I wanted to learn more about, had not been written about in books. Even as prominent musicians such as Junior Walker, did not have his story scribed in ink.

For that reason, much of my information was received through the dozens of personal interviews with the musicians, their family members, historians, and fans, who had fond memories and documentation that would prove valuable to my research.

Bobby Holley was my connection to the many artists featured in the book. Ernie Townsend came through with flying colors with his personal photos of the talent shows at Hamblin Community Center. Gregory Rose, who I have never met in person, was my internet connection to the world of Junior Walker (who may truly be Walker's biggest fan ever).

Mark Jason Murray of Film Fanatic.com provided photos for Jimmy Lynch and his years with Rudy Ray Moore films. Thanks go to Beth Howse of the Jubilee Singers historical collection for the classic photo, and to the New York Public Library for photos of Sy Oliver.

Victor Thomas was the first to share his photos and stories of days as an All Star. Bill Nicks, too, came through to share photos of his group, where Junior Walker got his start. Cal Street of *The Velvelettes*, assisted graciously in my quest to learn of Motown, which she has been a part of since she was in the ninth grade. She helped grant access at exclusive Motown events at the Roostertail in Detroit where I interviewed musicians who knew Junior Walker and other Battle Creek area artists.

Much of the historical contents and photos used here regarding the early history of African Americans in Battle Creek would not be as accessible (or in existence) had it not been for years of diligent research by Dorothy and Michael Martich. Their collection at Willard Library in Battle Creek, Michigan contains thousands of documents on African-American history This collection is priceless.

Melvin Evans contributed much of the personal history of the El Grotto Lounge, once owned by his sister, Helen and husband, Robert. Big thanks go to musician Jim Cummings who, in 2001, opened his home for the first meeting of the musicians for this book. Tico Taylor and those from the Frances Thornton Collection were invaluable with original photos and albums on the career of comedian Jimmy Lynch.

The archives of The *Battle Creek Enquirer,* where I worked as an editor during the time I discovered this story, was a treasure trove of original articles of interviews and obituaries.

Internet sources included Soullyoldies.com, and filmfanaddict.com. Books used include: *Temples of Sound: Inside the Great Recording Studios* by Jim Cogan and Williams Clark; and *Before Motown: The History of Jazz in Detroit 1920-1960* by Lars Bjorn and Jim Gallert.

Reader's Response for Here I Stand: One City's Musical History by Sonya Bernard-Hollins

The history of Battle Creek contains much more than I could publish in this one book. However, I hope the information shared throughout these pages will inspire others to learn about their own communities and the people, places, and events which contributed to its unique history.

To help motivate discussion regarding this book, I have enclosed a little quiz to see how much you remember. I encourage you to share what you have learned and even create your own quiz about Battle Creek music history!

Enjoy!

Did You Know....

1. What famous composer was born in Battle Creek in 1910, and went on to write hits for Frank Sinatra, Tommy Dorsey, and Jimmy Lunceford bands?

2. What drummer once played in a band that opened for such jazz greats as Miles Davis and Nancy Wilson?

3. What local activist auditioned for Motown but was later signed to Weis Records where he recorded, "Movin' Dancer"?

4. What duo called Battle Creek their home and later went on to write the song, "Someday We'll Be Together," for the Supremes?

5. What Battle Creek club was the song, "Shotgun," created?

6. What group recorded the timeless hit, "What Does it Take to Win Your Love?"

7. What R&B recording artist from Battle Creek was the first act signed to LaFace Records?

8. What Battle Creek Gospel singer worked for the governor of Georgia?

9. What Battle Creek artist recorded his first hit while still in high school at Battle Creek Central?

10. What Grammy-award winning musician first performed at the El Grotto when he was too young to get into the club?

Selective Index

E

F

G

H

K

L

M

Q

Quakers	4, 7

R

Rainbow Room, The	42, 133
Ravens, The	80
Redding, Otis	112
Reid, L.A.	140
Rhythm Rockers	87, 92-93
Richardson, Bruce	96-97
Riley, Eric	141, 143
Robinson, Jackie	27
Royal, Billy Joe	75
Royaliers	79
Rupert Harris Band	122

S

Scott, Sherry	77-78
Shifters, The	71-74, 129
"Shotgun" (song)	81, 85, 90-91, 95-97, 129, 136, 151
Simpkins, Andy	120, 122
Sinatra, Frank	41-42, 151
Slavery	3-5, 7-9, 11, 15, 17, 24, 57
Snyder, Thomas	26-27, 32
Southeastern Junior High	71
Spinks, Leon	71
Stax Records	111-112, 135, 151
Stevenson, Mickey	104, 111
Stewart, Jim	112
Stitt, Sonny	96, 122
Sweet, Jim	82

About the Authors

Sean and Sonya Hollins are the owners of Season Press LLC, a publishing and editorial consulting firm located in West Michigan. The couple has helped dozens make their dream of becoming an author a reality. Together they also operate Fortitude Graphic Design and Printing, and *Community Voices* Magazine.

Sean brings more than 20 years of award-winning creativity as a graphic artist and photographer to their companies while Sonya brings more than 20 years of experience as an award-winning journalist. In addition to *Here I Stand* the Hollins' have written and published together the children's book, *Benjamin Losford and His Handy Dandy Clippers*, *The Journey: My Blessings Journal,* and *Our Michigan Women: 30 Women from the Michigan Women's Hall of Fame*.

They have four children and a dog, Max.

Made in the USA
Middletown, DE
19 October 2022

13105184R00099